WINGNUT'S COMPLETE
SURFING

Robert "Wingnut" Weaver
with Scott Bannerot

International Marine / McGraw-Hill

Camden, Maine   New York   Chicago   San Francisco   Lisbon   London   Madrid
Mexico City   Milan   New Delhi   San Juan   Seoul   Singapore   Sydney   Toronto

The **McGraw-Hill** Companies

Library of Congress Cataloging-in-Publication Data

Weaver, Robert "Wingnut."
    Wingnut's complete surfing / Robert "Wingnut" Weaver with Scott Bannerot.
       p.   cm.
    Includes bibliographical references and index.
    ISBN 0-07-149706-4
    1. Surfing.   I. Bannerot, Scott P., 1959–   .   II. Title.

  GV840.S8W43   2009
  797.3'2—dc22   2008049165

1 2 3 4 5 6 7 8 9 10 11 12 13 14 15 16 17 18 19 20 21 22 DOC/DOC 0 9

ISBN   978-0-07-149706-0
MHID   0-07-149706-4

Interior design by Think Design LLC

McGraw-Hill books are available at special quantity discounts to use as premiums and sales promotions or for use in corporate training programs. To contact a representative, please visit the Contact Us pages at www.mhprofessional.com.

This book is printed on acid-free paper.

For Janice and Cameron

—WINGNUT

**For Ryan and Robyn, to the memory of Fred Austin,
and to the memory of Sash Spencer**

—SCOTT

Contents

Preface

I love surfing! That seems like an obvious statement to start with, but it's not just the act of surfing that I love—it's absolutely everything involved with being a surfer. From the moment I caught my first wave and experienced that sensation of riding on top of the water, for a brief moment feeling as if I had mastered the power of the ocean and somehow tricked it into doing my bidding, I was hooked. But surfing now is so much more to me than just riding waves. I love to watch everyone surf, watch little kids play on foamies in the whitewater, watch moms and dads take lessons with their kids. I love how the kids are always better than their parents, and I love that the parents are not only at peace with that but proud of it. I love to watch the ocean transform as a storm rolls into the coast, how it morphs into a wild maelstrom of wind, waves, and foam.

I was fortunate enough to grow up near the beach. The ocean has been a part of my summers and afternoons for as long as I can remember, and sharing it with others has become my career and my passion. Surfing is an extremely selfish pursuit. Rarely does the act of catching a wave benefit anyone other than the surfer. But the feeling that the ride gives you, the stoke, gets loaded into your system for you to draw on for hours or days after. This reserve of stoke allows one to be a better, nicer human back on dry land.

That is why I love to teach people how to surf—because in so doing, I am showing them how to share in the magic that the ocean has to offer. I have run surf programs in America and Europe and have taken pro football players and A-list celebrities out for their first surf lessons. Rich or poor, CEO or mail-room clerk, famous or not, it doesn't matter. Surfing is the great equalizer, and I have seen on every one of my students' faces that same childlike thrill and wonder the first time they ride a wave.

But best of all has been teaching my son. My wife, Janice, was already learning when we met, so I can't take credit for getting her started. But during the two years we lived in Hawaii she became a very smooth and stylish surfer, and I like to take a little credit for that. Now that the whole family can paddle out together, laugh, and argue about whose turn it is, it's a dream come true.

A few years back, at a surf festival in Australia, I met Scott Bannerot, a world-class sailor and fisherman and a newly converted surfer. His stoke was electric, and his son was a younger version of mine. He told me about a fishing book he had written while sailing the globe, and he said he wanted to write a book on surfing. While I have taught hundreds of people to surf and have made some instructional movies that I am very proud of, writing a book myself was a daunting prospect. In Scott I knew I had found the ideal coauthor. He and I talked and surfed and e-mailed, and the concepts for this book were written, discussed, and worried over, and now here it is.

Scott has done a great job explaining the challenges, nuances, and art that go into the act of surfing, and he has done a great job combining our two views. Sometimes it's easier for a relative newcomer to a sport to give the basics a clearer explanation. My role has been to backstop Scott on the basics and to guide the instruction through intermediate techniques.

I am so impressed with Scott's work and very proud to be a part of this book. I hope that it will help you enjoy the ocean—and life—as only lucky surfers can.

Aloha,
Wingnut

Acknowledgments

Many thanks to our contributing photographers: Mitsuyuki Shibata, Hitoshi "Tochi" Sato, Marcelo Matos, Aaron Fisher, Robyn McIntyre, Matthew Bambling, Wendy Bannerot, Paea Tavake, Herb McCormick, and Skip and Cyd Nielsen. I'd also like to especially thank George Cockle and the entire staff of the *Wingnut's Art of Longboarding* project for their contributions to this book, particularly Kenji Sasamoto, Takashi Isobe, Toshiro Izawa, and Hideyuki Takahashi.

Many top surfers contributed to this work along the way. Thanks particularly to Joel Tudor and Dino Miranda for their input. My wife, Janice, strongly supported and contributed to this project, as she does all my endeavors. She and our son, Cameron, are the best teammates I could ever imagine, in surfing and in life.

Scott and I thank Jon Eaton and Molly Mulhern at International Marine for all of their support and work on this project, especially in keeping the faith through assorted transitions. Thanks also to Julia Anderson Bauer at McGraw-Hill for her patience and dedication to detail.

—Wingnut

Eric Vogt, Michael H. Owens, T. C. Cardillo, Paul McGrew, Tom Morkin, Andrew and Chris Krajacic, Craig Nickalls, Jack Glanville, Jerry Ault, Peter "Stumpy" Wallace, Marty Simpson, Tim Simpson, Gavin Platz, Skip and Cyd Nielsen, Herb McCormick, Dave Byrne (with special thanks for the surfboard repair tips and information), "Big Nick," and a bunch of other smiling, spirited surfers I know more by appearance than names, have each contributed to this book without realizing it. Special thanks also to all of the young guys and girls and families in Australia for inspiring, encouraging, and surfing with Ryan and me, like Clay Davis; Ashley McLaughlin; Brad and Harry Gill; Dylan and Tom Moore; Maggie McCormick; Ellie, Chloe, and Harry Graves; Mitchell Cole; Jack Browning; Connor Boland; Luke Karajic; Jack Weule; and easily the most stoked surfing buddy we have, fourteen-year-old Max Lacey, who rides his bike miles to surf each morning at the crack of dawn before school, and with whom we surf frequently by boat and by truck, in all conditions. The only ones who might threaten his title are Ryan's cousins, Simon and Olivia Bannerot, and their dad Steve Bannerot, all from Seattle, who just started surfing this week on a visit to Australia.

I'd like to especially thank Tim Queeney, Peter Jenkins, and Herb McCormick for their friendship, advice, and support of my writing. Special friends Heather, Melissa, and Sam Gill; Bevan, Kimbra, Laura, and Mackenzie O'Keeffe; Jacob Parsons-O'Keeffe; Janelle and Tom Boland; Jason and Debbie Graves; Daniel Scott; and Peter Davis have all assisted over the course of the project.

My wife, Dr. Robyn McIntyre, who supplied valuable medical information and photography for the book; who largely made possible, in many ways, my participation in this project; and who constantly inspires with her intelligence, wisdom, and zest for surfing, sailing, diving, and life in general. Robyn and Ryan are a stalwart surfing team, and they're also the most dedicated, honest, loving, and supportive family one could ever wish for.

The love and support of Steve Bannerot; Leslie Leopold; Lynn Kohr; Palmer and Betty Ann Bannerot; Joanne, Juliet, Olivia, Simon, Rick, and Eric Bannerot; Marshall, Sage, Cedar, and Stratton Kohr; Steve, Annie, and Ellie Leopold; and Paul, Norma, Jack, Sue, Sam, John, Mark, and Marie Glanville; Jill Hanrahan; Jody Wolf; and Carolyn Brink is an embarrassment of riches.

Very special thanks to Ryan Bannerot. We've stuck together through thick and thin, clean glassy days with the sun shining, others rough and stormy with hard onshore winds. His personal toughness, kindness, courage, good humor, buoyancy, sense of joy about life, and, most of all, his loyalty, reign supreme.

—Scott

Introduction

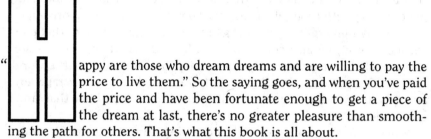

by Scott Bannerot

"Happy are those who dream dreams and are willing to pay the price to live them." So the saying goes, and when you've paid the price and have been fortunate enough to get a piece of the dream at last, there's no greater pleasure than smoothing the path for others. That's what this book is all about.

Surfing was one of my childhood dreams, but circumstances got in the way of realizing that dream until I was closing in on forty. I'm still just an enthusiastic amateur at best, but no one in the world has more fun surfing than I do. This is the book I needed when I was struggling to learn surfing in remote Pacific locations with very little advice. I got absolutely hammered and made every mistake there is to make. When I finally got it all going on sandy beach breaks in eastern Australia, I vowed to help create the book that would capture the essence of what one needs to know and save others from what I went through.

Someone who must struggle to succeed, like a student who works long and hard to make a B, is often able to explain things effectively to other struggling students. That's my role in this book. Having learned to surf so recently, I remember every baffling roadblock and every "aha!" moment along the way. If you're a beginning surfer, I think I can anticipate your questions, and the answers are in this book.

Then again, if you find the right brilliant professor, someone who not only is performing at the top of his or her game but also can put things into clear terms for the rest of us, you have the best of all worlds. That is why I'm so ecstatic that Robert "Wingnut" Weaver is the lead author of this book.

For many thousands of surfers over the past forty-plus years, it all began with Bruce Brown's classic 1964 movie, *Endless Summer*. No other production more completely captured the imagination or more thoroughly inspired, educated, and just plain thrilled people about surfing. When, thirty years later, Bruce outdid himself and produced the 1994 classic *Endless Summer II*, he neatly tied together the past, present, and future of surfing, firing up a whole new generation of surfers and rekindling the flame for his original fans. Wingnut, age twenty-six and twenty-seven during the filming and one of the world's best surfers, turned in an energetic and unique performance that contributed heavily to the groundswell of praise for this movie. Wingnut surfed a longboard side by side with the world's best high-performance shortboard riders, contrasting their frenetic style with the smooth grace of the more traditional and more versatile longboard. More important, his devotion and skill to the surfing equipment that nearly all surfers learn on and many prefer to stay with brought surfing back down to earth. And more important still, Wingnut didn't just surf giant waves in exotic locales that most will never visit; he also surfed, beautifully and inspirationally, the sort of waves that break constantly at everyday locations all over the world. Despite his obviously high skill level, his approach allowed average guys and gals to say, "Hey, I could do that. I could ride a board like that, and I could ride that wave."

Since that starring role, and continuing through a decade and a half of teaching, surf guiding, movie making, and promoting the sport, Wingnut has taught and inspired countless numbers of people all over the world—young and old, women, men, and children—about the pure joy of surfing.

My son, Ryan, and I must have watched *Endless Summer II* a hundred times together as we sailed across the Pacific on our forty-one-foot sloop. Eventually we holed up in eastern Australia, and from there we could hear waves breaking on the lovely sand beaches on which part of the movie was filmed. Nine years old now, Ryan learned to surf when he was three, and one of his favorite things to do in his first six years of surfing has been to pretend that he is either Wingnut or costar Pat O'Connell (depending these days on whether he is surfing his custom longboard or his custom shortboard). So Ryan was, if anything, even more excited than I one balmy October morning as we rumbled southward past Brisbane in an aging Toyota Land Cruiser, our bow pointed toward Coolangatta, on the Gold Coast, and our first meeting with Wingnut about writing this book. Ryan's questions were never ending. "Will he look like he does in the movie?" "Will he talk to me?" "Do you think he'll like me?"

Soon afterward Ryan and I were sitting at a table poolside with Wingnut and surfing legends Robert August and Wayne Lynch. Wingnut bought Ryan some potato wedges and took a photo of him to e-mail back to his own son, Cameron. While the adults drank coffee, Ryan wolfed down the wedges and dove into the pool, then started flying down the slide backward and sideways, crashing into the water to the laughter of the surfing icons. Robert and Wayne drifted off after a bit, and Wingnut and I began discussing this book, and surfing, in earnest. I learned more about surfing in forty-five minutes from his soft-spoken, humorous insights and anecdotes than I had the previous forty-seven years, and I knew right then that this project was going to work.

"Surfing is a humbling sport. Even at the highest levels, you can have a spectacular ride, yet on the very next wave fall off and look like someone who is just starting out," said Wingnut. Perhaps it's that aspect of surfing, or perhaps it's that people at the top of an endeavor often tend to be far humbler than some of their less accomplished colleagues, but I was struck by the offhand, selfless modesty displayed by Wingnut, Robert, and Wayne that day at Coolangatta. They were far more interested in hearing about my sailing adventures than talking about themselves.

The fastest way to experience surfing is to choose the right equipment, arm yourself with fundamental knowledge about what to do, get yourself out there, paddle onto the face of the right wave, pop up from prone to standing position, ride the wave, and safely disengage. There's nothing else like it. Very quickly you'll want more details on how to turn, maneuver, nose ride, tube ride, and take on bigger and more challenging waves. A competent, comprehensive, inspirational, clearly written, well-illustrated account of how to do all of these things, infused with (but not obscured by) entertaining stories and anecdotes—which are much easier to remember than dry warnings and step-by-step instructions—can not only provide that first big boost toward success, but also go on serving as your primary reference while you advance to bigger waves and more advanced maneuvers. Even the pros can pick up knowledge and insights from listening to another pro.

Granted, you can't learn to surf simply by reading a book, but reading the *right* book can save you a great deal of wasted effort and frustration, protect you from many pitfalls (including physical harm), and vastly accelerate your learning curve, all of which translate into having the most possible fun in the shortest possible time. That, in a nutshell, is the purpose of this book.

Most surfers begin by gazing at photos and watching footage of skilled surfers riding huge, hollow, dangerous waves. We don't see the waves this same surfer missed, or the times he or she was thrown over the lip of a wave like a rag doll, or the failed *pop-ups* (quickly going from prone to standing position) and resulting crashes. We don't even see the surfer paddle onto the wave. We certainly don't see the surfer on his or her first ride, wobbling around like a newborn colt and falling off the board. All we see is an expert crouched gracefully, swooping down an incredible aqua wall and shooting off on a long, perfect ride. And we all ask ourselves the same questions: Could I do that? What will it take to become the rider on that board, screaming gleefully down that wave?

The answers to those questions depend on a lot of things, including your age and physical condition, the amount of time and energy you are able to devote to the endeavor, and the opportunities you have or can make available for the quest. But the basic answer is yes—whether you are seven or seventy, you can do this. You can paddle out through the surf on the right board and with the right gear, pick a suitable wave, position yourself on that wave, feel the board begin to take off, push off the board to a standing position, and feel the power, joy, and exhilaration of surfing. You can do it easily within your first hour, and from there you can take it to whatever level suits your circumstances. If you keep doing it consistently over time, you will be in superb physical condition, and you will feel mentally relaxed and refreshed to a degree unfamiliar to most people on the planet. Those are facts, and the result is an incredible foundation for whatever else you do in life.

Wingnut's Complete Surfing begins by distilling the essentials for the fastest, most pain-free possible progress to your first experience of flying along on a wave, and then takes you far beyond to the pro-level nuances and secrets of one of the best surfers in the world. Along the way we address every important topic—surfing history, physical oceanography, surfboard technology, safety, surf sociology, gear alternatives and sources, and more. I hope and believe that this collaboration between an average beginning surfer (me!) and a high-flying pro and superb teacher will give you just what you need to realize *your* surfing dreams.

Surfing Success

A PREVIEW

by Scott Bannerot

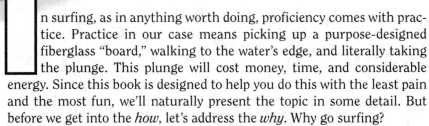

In surfing, as in anything worth doing, proficiency comes with practice. Practice in our case means picking up a purpose-designed fiberglass "board," walking to the water's edge, and literally taking the plunge. This plunge will cost money, time, and considerable energy. Since this book is designed to help you do this with the least pain and the most fun, we'll naturally present the topic in some detail. But before we get into the *how*, let's address the *why*. Why go surfing?

Can you remember, as a child, giving yourself wholly to the pursuit of an activity that brought you joy? It might have been swimming, shooting baskets, fishing, or some more sedentary activity, but while you were engaged in it hours would melt away unnoticed. When we come of age and in all likelihood are forced to spend an inordinate amount of time earning money, we forget the timeless joy of undistracted engagement in an activity pursued for its own sake. We forget how to play.

Surfing takes you back there. It makes you feel like a kid again. Even for the average, garden-variety participant, surfing is such a unique synthesis of physical exercise and conditioning, intellectual stimulation, and immersion in natural beauty, and is just so downright happy and thrilling, few who experience it can ever let it go. Surfing makes your soul smile.

Defining Success

Whether you start playing the guitar, taking golf lessons, training for marathons, acting, writing, learning martial arts, or participating on a sports team, you usually have an ultimate goal, conscious or unconscious, and you keep running and rerunning a cost-benefit analysis relative to that goal—prospective pain versus prospective gain. When will you consider yourself successful? When you receive an award, a trophy, or public acclaim?

Surfing is hardly immune from this sort of thinking, but success in surfing is fundamentally different. Maybe this is because of surfing's malleable, highly fluid nature and the fact that success is so completely defined by the participant. Surfing is an intensely personal activity—just you, your board, and a wave. Every day is different. All you have to do is catch the wave, stand up, ride, and do it again . . . three times, five times, ten times. You win. It doesn't matter whether you're surfing a one-foot wave on a sandy beach break or a roaring hollow monster at Pipeline on Oahu's famed North Shore. Cameron Weaver and Ryan Bannerot started before their third birthdays. Many continue into their seventies, a few into their nineties. It's the cheapest life insurance around. Success is measured purely by the personal happiness you generate. There is no obligation to impress others, win accolades, or even worry about what anyone else thinks.

This makes surfing about as close to pure fun as our species can approach on this particular planet. Other crazes come and go, yet the popularity of surfing has never waned since the modern worldwide explosion that began in the 1960s. There's a wave out there for everyone—every generation, race, and gender—and each surfer comes out a winner. Success in surfing is wrapped up in that infectious attitude of making every day great over the largest possible variety of conditions.

And in the Beginning . . .

Watching a superstar perform often triggers questions about how it all began. Wingnut grew up in Newport Beach, California, not far from a fairly consistent and reasonably friendly break known as Blackie's, between the Newport Beach Pier and a rock jetty. While he had boogie boarded and body surfed since a young age, he didn't actually surf on a board until age sixteen, not long before his seventeenth birthday, during the summer between his junior and senior years in high school. He was on the high school wrestling team, weighing in at a mere 115 pounds, and his coach lent him a 1960s-era "log" in the form of a forty-pound Dave Sweet longboard. Wingnut took to it instantly. Already accustomed to the hard part—catching a wave—he started out by paddling vigorously onto the first few waves, and after experiencing the thrill of popping up and standing as the big board surged along at an angle to the shore a few times, he was hooked. Thousands of waves and twenty-five years later he can't actually recall the very first wave, just the feeling that it was something he'd always do. Needless to say, his wrestling coach never saw the board again, and Wingnut became a regular at Blackie's, often grabbing a ride with his next-door neighbor, a surfer who was also a firefighter. He has never looked back.

At six years Wingnut's senior but with a lifetime wave count that will never put a scratch in his, I can easily recall my first wave. I attended junior high and high school near Pittsburgh, Pennsylvania (to this day undiscovered for surfing), and once participated in an exciting family beach vacation to Fenwick Island, Delaware. It was 1972, I was thirteen, and although I'd seen *Endless Summer* some years earlier and had the dream, it wasn't until I saw my cousin Jack Glanville out in some small waves, sitting expectantly on a kid-sized Corky Carroll egg-style board, that I knew I was going to get a first shot. I was out beside Jack in a flash, where I learned that he hadn't been able to stand up yet but that I could have a go. Beside myself with excitement, I paddled onto the first foaming white breaker, every bit of twelve inches tall, stood up shakily, wobbled in, and T-boned the beach moments later. Neither of us could believe it. Surfing was no problem; I had it down. Little did I know that that would be my best ride for the next twenty-three years.

The Worst Record in Surfing History

While Wingnut was rapidly honing his skills in California, I was accumulating what just might be the worst record in surfing history. In case anyone doubts me when I say that if I can surf, you can too, perhaps it's worth recounting the highlights from that record:

~ **Summer of 1975, Waikiki, Oahu, Hawaii.** I've been invited by high school friend Roy Stang to accompany him on a supercheap trip to Hawaii with his parents and a large group of elderly people. When Roy and I rent boards and paddle out into the surf, we notice right away that the two Hawaiian guys catching graceful rides on the long, slow swells have boards much longer than ours, but we don't worry about it. Instead we paddle ourselves silly trying to catch waves on our rented shortboards, and we catch nary a one. We leave the beach feeling sad and defeated. As Wingnut's friend, surfing legend Mickey Munoz, says, "There are no bad waves, just bad equipment choices."

~ **Spring of 1986, Rincon, Puerto Rico.** With a few days to kill between trips on a high-seas swordfish longliner, I rent a car and strike out for what I've heard is a world-class surf spot to get the monkey off my back once and for all. Pretty little *right-handers* (waves that peel to your right when your back is to them and you're facing the beach) are breaking in a beginner-friendly area, but once more the only rental boards available are shortboards. Gamely paddling onto wave after wave, I experience hours of failure in every imaginable form, but not one ride. As I walk bedraggled down the street to return the board, an aging overweight surfer accosts me. "Man," he says, "I've never seen anyone try so hard. I felt so bad watching you. You've got the wrong board to learn on. That thing is way too small. You've got to get on a longboard and you'll be off to a real good start, no problem. Then, if you want, you can move down to something smaller and more specialized."

⁓ **Late 1994, Miami, Florida.** While I'm preparing my forty-one-foot sloop *Elan* to sail to the Pacific, my friend Dr. Jerry Ault implores me to take a surfboard or two. "You've *got* to take at least one board," he says. "You're sailing to some of the best surf spots in the world." The surfing dream, tattered and faded, is still there, but I'm so overloaded with gear and boat issues that I never get around to acquiring boards.

⁓ **August 1995, Taapuna, Tahiti, and Haapiti, Moorea, Society Islands.** With *Elan* anchored in lagoons inside these world-class reef breaks, I'm visited by longtime friend and surfer Dr. Mike Owens. He and I motor out in the inflatable dinghy to give surfing a try. In addition to his own board, Mike has brought with him an old single-fin short-board for me to use. It barely floats me, and for me the experience is just another replay of right waves, wrong equipment. The waves at Taapuna are quite small and manageable, while the Haapiti surf is nothing less than an epic, perfectly curling *double overhead* (wave faces twice the height of a standing surfer). I can only watch in total frustration as other guys—but not me—catch wave after wave at both spots.

⁓ **Early 1996, anchored at Christmas Island, Republic of Kiribati.** A chance meeting with Hawaii-based surfer Eric Vogt leads to some detailed instruction, and Eric sends me an 8′2″ funboard when he gets back to Kauai. After a few absolute poundings and a lot of wipeouts at the reef break by the main pass, the day I've been dreaming of finally arrives—four rides in a row on smallish glassy swells. My pop-ups are not the quickest or smoothest, and I execute no turns or maneuvers, but these are bona fide rides, and I'm in heaven. Soon after, however, mere hours after *Elan* returns to Nuku Hiva in the Marquesas Islands, someone swims out and steals the board off the deck.

⁓ **September 1996.** When Eric flies to Pago Pago, American Samoa, to help me sail *Elan* to New Zealand, he brings a 7′5″ *gun*, which is a big-wave shortboard. He leaves it with me as a gift, telling me to hang on to this one and threatening to return and take it back if I don't get out there and use it. I make some progress at sandy beach breaks over the next four years but often watch longboarders whizzing by on wave after wave while I only catch one once in a while. I also try to take on heavier conditions ill-suited to my low skill level, with poor results.

⁓ **First half of 2001, Republic of the Marshall Islands.** While *Elan* is moored in Majuro, traveling surfer/sailors T. C. Cardillo and Paul McGrew take me to a couple of reef breaks with challenging conditions, and I can't get anywhere with the 7′5″ gun. They advise me to back up a step and surf a longboard in conditions that permit me to pop up and get some quality time standing and riding, and only then think about tougher conditions. It's the same advice I received from the aging surfer in Puerto Rico fifteen years earlier—a measure of my intervening progress. T. C. and Paul highly recommend the epoxy Tuflite boards from Surftech for their strength and durability. These boards, they say, will survive ocean passages on the deck of a sailboat. They also strongly recommend the split-toe boots a surfer wears around sharp coral. (I am trying to surf with dive boots at this time.)

- **Early 2002, Pago Pago, American Samoa.** I finally decide to do this thing properly before I die of old age. With the help of Robert August, Wingnut, Surftech, and the Hawaiian shop Surf-N-Sea, I order the Surftech versions of a 9'6" Robert August What I Ride longboard and an 8' Randy French Hybrid. I also order split-toe boots, rash guards, leashes, proper board bags by FCS, spare fins . . . the works.

- **September 2002, Malololailai Island, Fiji.** While I care for my ill first wife and my three-year-old son Ryan, the new boards have yet to get wet. Accosting me at the Musket Cove Bar, young surfer/sailors Andrew and Chris Krajacic inform me that I need to be ready the next day at 5:00 A.M., as they'll be swinging by to take me to Wilke's Pass, just north of famed Tavarua. Drew helps me wax up the longboard and install the fins. My total score is one wipeout on a pretty big wave, but I can sense I'm getting closer.

- **January 2003 to the present, eastern Australia.** Despite two long work sojourns back home in Florida, *Elan*'s base on the Sunshine Coast of Queensland finally affords the perfect combination of lovely point breaks and sandy beach breaks. Possessing the right gear and the enthusiasm of a little kid at Christmas, I enjoy consistently successful surfing at last.

So What's It Really Like?

Wingnut describes the thrill of surfing as well as anyone. He describes it, for example, in the beginning of his three-part DVD series *Wingnut's Art of Longboarding,* which I regard as a must-have (and if you just can't wait for shipping of the DVDs, you can instantly download them to your iPod or iTunes library from thesurfnetwork.com). It's that timeless thrill of the downhill ride—often experienced and perhaps best and most purely appreciated as young kids—on a skateboard, snowboard, skis, bicycle, or sled. It's a dazzling rush down the slope that you want to experience again and again, so much so that you'll take risks and go to great lengths to do it, to the point of utter exhaustion. Speeding down and across that smooth, unbroken wave face, your mind is focused on something pristine, dynamic, captivating, refreshing, titillating, all-encompassing.

An added bonus is that, most of the time, suitable breaking waves adorn picturesque wild environments—beaches, rugged promontories and shorelines, oceanic reefs, passes, and islands. You paddle back in to shore from a great surf outing, step out of the water, board under your arm, and there's usually no place you'd rather be and no people you'd rather be with. In short, there's no place like here, no time like now.

I've already contrasted Wingnut's smooth cruise into surfing success with my own far humbler and thornier path—a path that this book is designed to prevent you from traveling. No matter the path, however, the destination is similar. So let me tell you what that destination felt like for me when I finally reached it. Just as the soul group En Vogue introduced their live version of "This Is Your Life" a while back, "it goes a little something like this."

I was pedaling along on my bike, transporting my then three-year-old son Ryan southward along the beach road to preschool from the marina where *Elan* was docked. This ride was our morning ritual. Perched on his kiddie seat, Ryan chattered happily. I could hear the roar of heavy surf—a sound almost as compelling as my son's glad stream of words—but I was focused on my mission. After dropping off Ryan, I swung over to have a look. Huge, back-lit aqua breakers were *closing out* the entire beach front (collapsing along lengthy sections, making them very difficult to ride comfortably or at all). Yet I knew the rocky promontory to the north would be a different story, so off I went, my excitement growing. I rode up to the lighthouse on the cliff and gaped at the enormous swells wrapping around the point. A few surfers were dropping down the massive, near-vertical wave faces, then shooting off on spectacular rides.

I got to thinking. Yes, certainly these surfers were mostly either better or far better than I, but there had to have been a day when they took the big plunge. I'd frequently ridden my bike along the river inlet jetty that faced the incoming surfers. Weeks before, I'd finally grown tired of being an onlooker and, on a day of small to medium waves, had taken the step up from safe sandy beach breaks to the steep peeling waves and rocky bottom of this particular point break. Now the monster breakers in front of me were crashing along similarly to waves I'd ridden here before. Granted, these waves were much, much bigger, but the mechanics of paddling onto a wave face and popping up would be the same. The main difference between the surfers below and me was that they were doing it and I wasn't. I made the decision to go for it.

I pedaled back to the marina, hopped aboard *Elan*, and made ready—donned a wetsuit, waxed the board, unlocked the dinghy, and cranked up the outboard. I'd decided to take the 9′6″ Robert August longboard, since it had served me so well for every step up I'd taken in surfing, just as T. C. and Paul had said it would. A stable platform that easily catches waves means less to control and worry about, freeing the rider to concentrate on the new aspects of whatever he or she is taking on. Plus, I knew from watching Wingnut in *Endless Summer II* that a longboard could definitely surf these big waves very well, at least with the right pilot at the controls. And, as Wingnut later pointed out to me, my familiarity with the break and the board was critical.

I rounded the bend in the Mooloolah River with butterflies in my stomach. Those butterflies rose in a pronounced flutter when an enormous breaker cascaded across the entire mouth of the inlet in front of me. The expert surfer riding that swell was dwarfed by it. I had a sudden impulse to turn around then and there, but I pushed that notion away. Motoring out through the surf zone during the next lull, I swung around to anchor far outside the break.

The waves that had appeared so large from the cliff top looked colossal from sea level. I felt small and alone, my pucker meter definitely pegged. I wished someone was with me, if for no other reason than to recover my body and take it to my family. Then I looked over at the spectators clustered along the jetty and decided I was sick of being in that crowd. I reminded myself that each one of these surfers had experienced a first time. They had survived, and so would I. I even had a realistic chance of success.

I dropped the board in the water, fastened the leash, jumped on, and began paddling. Huge green mountains swelled up as they marched around the rocky headland, exploding in white fury on the rocks. The deep-throated roar of the crashing break was like thunder. Offshore wind gusts whipped spray backward off the towering crests, creating miniature rainbows in the sunlight. The few surfers out there were young—considerably younger than I—and chiseled. Equipped with high-performance shortboards, they were screaming and cheering the wild take-offs of their buddies on immense wave faces. It was like strapping on the pads and running out under the stadium lights for a football game—or, more accurately, like wobbling out on a cane while younger, fitter players rushed out around you. No turning back now.

I stroked my way beyond and just offshore of the small knot of surfers and paused off the *corner* of the take-off zone, wide and outside. I'd no sooner turned to look out to sea when a gigantic mass of green-tinted water humped up and approached with alarming speed, rising as it advanced. I took a deep breath, turned, and started paddling at an angle to the wave face, nose pointed for deeper water, away from the rocky shore and break zone. "Stay cool, stay cool," I said to myself as the board picked up speed and began to slide faster and faster down the increasingly steep slope. A careful, balanced pop-up—arms straight, left knee driven forward and up under the chest, rising in one motion to a bent-knee standing position—and I was racing diagonally down a wave face easily two times the length of the board, so steep now, and dropping so fast, that my stomach rose in my abdomen, the roar of white water close behind.

I whizzed by other surfers in the lineup, wondering vaguely why they all broke into smiles. (Clearly they had no idea of the mortal danger they were in with me at the controls.) The ride went on and on, the fast tickety-tack of ripples slapping underfoot while white spray shot out from the racing board. Suddenly the end of the jetty was looming to my left, and the wave started to fatten, the velocity of the board easing. I realized that the silly, unconscious grin pasted across my face was so wide my skin was stretched tight. I shot past the jetty and finally swung up and over the last of the wave crest some three hundred yards from where I'd taken off.

The elation of that moment is something I will always remember and for which I will be eternally grateful. It was a long time coming, the consummation of a lifetime dream. I knew I'd been very lucky to catch the right part of the right wave on my first attempt. I had no illusions about how much I had to learn. I hadn't taken off deep and steep; I hadn't done any maneuvers. Importantly, I'd ridden out toward the shoulder of a fat, forgiving wave section, along a zone of deeper water, so the wave had been safe despite its size and velocity. Nevertheless, that ride changed me forever. Six rides later, including two collapsing wave segments (close-outs) that threw me far under for quite some time, those waves no longer seemed intimidating.

This is no war story—rides like these are nothing for even an intermediate surfer. The point is, if someone with my humble pedigree can do it, most anyone can. Here's hoping the same thing will happen to you. For Wingnut, all of the ingredients for success were close at hand, and it's fair to say that a combination of extraordinary talent, opportunity, and circumstance translated naturally and smoothly into superstardom. As you've seen, I'm at the opposite end of the spectrum. You'd have to go to great efforts to duplicate my trials and tribulations in surfing. To this day I still suffer moments of looking like an uncoordinated idiot. Yet racing along those lovely wave faces, I'm inhabiting the same watery heaven that shines on Wingnut Weaver. You won't have much trouble attaining my mediocre skill level, yet I can tell you I'm having a blast. I will never approach Wingnut's grace and skill, but that is irrelevant. I feel the same thing he feels—that timeless thrill of the surfing experience. You can feel it too.

Getting Started

A COMPLETE MINI-PRIMER

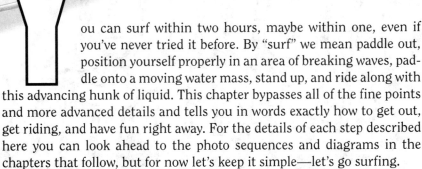

2

You can surf within two hours, maybe within one, even if you've never tried it before. By "surf" we mean paddle out, position yourself properly in an area of breaking waves, paddle onto a moving water mass, stand up, and ride along with this advancing hunk of liquid. This chapter bypasses all of the fine points and more advanced details and tells you in words exactly how to get out, get riding, and have fun right away. For the details of each step described here you can look ahead to the photo sequences and diagrams in the chapters that follow, but for now let's keep it simple—let's go surfing.

While this book is mostly about surfing on surfboards, which is the normal understanding of the term *surfing*, you should know that people use many other kinds of equipment to ride waves. These include kayaks, windsurfers, kite surfers, kneeboards, rescue boards, skimboards, paddle boards, assorted boats, Jet Skis, WaveRunners, wave skis, surf skis, outrigger canoes, plain human bodies, and, significantly, boogie boards (also called body boards) and stand-up paddle (SUP) surfboards (see Appendix A). Of all these different ways to ride a wave, none is more effective or readily learned than the boogie board, and we recommend it not only as an excellent starting point for surfing but also as a fun alternative to stand-up board riding.

A boogie board is less than half the body length of its rider, a shapely foam affair held under the torso and maneuvered by leaning and tilting with the help of hand pressure and position. You'll want to purchase a boogie board, boogie-boarding swim fins, protective neoprene or polypropylene socks, keeper straps for the fins, and a leash for the board (which attaches to the biceps or wrist). If you don't own board shorts or a rash guard (a long- or short-sleeved polypropylene shirt), get those too, and if the water is cold you'll need a wetsuit.

Head to a sandy beach with smallish breaking waves, suit up, and wade out into the water. Lie chest down on the boogie board and begin propelling yourself away from the shore by kicking with the fins. You can also stroke, freestyle, with your arms. When you encounter an oncoming wave, *duck dive* by pushing down on the front of the boogie board—sticking your butt up and head down—just before the wave arrives (Figure 2.1). This pushes you beneath the rushing swell. Now arch your back and ascend, head up, with your board angled toward the surface. You've circumvented the shoreward surge of the wave and have prevented yourself

FIGURE 2.1 Starting with a boogie board.

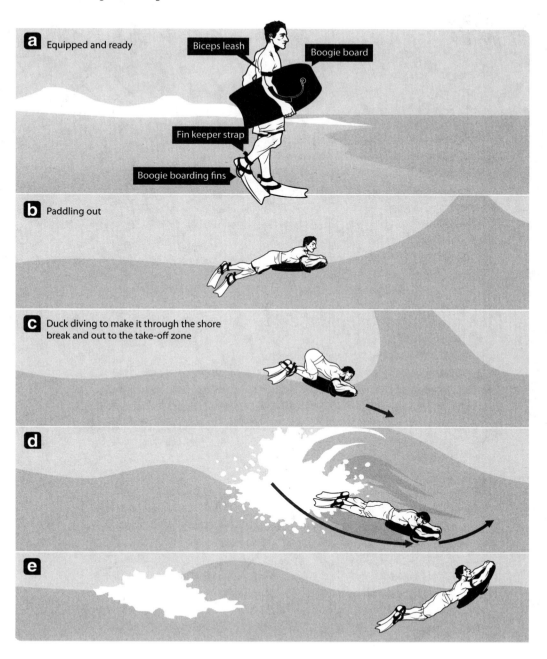

a Equipped and ready

Biceps leash

Boogie board

Fin keeper strap

Boogie boarding fins

b Paddling out

c Duck diving to make it through the shore break and out to the take-off zone

d

e

Ariel Medel

FIGURE 2.2 Using ranges to stay in the best spot.

Beach

Ariel Medel

from losing ground, and now you are back to making your way out beyond the breakers to the *take-off zone,* that area where swells encounter the bottom and elevate before breaking.

When you get to this area, stop and wait. Line up two objects on shore a little to your left, and do the same looking off a bit to your right to accurately mark your spot—this process of aligning objects is called *finding a range* (Figure 2.2). (In clear water you may be able to orient to a distinct coral head or other bottom feature as well.) As a wave approaches, turn toward the beach and kick your fins to get some momentum. You will feel yourself pick up speed as the energy of the wave propels you with it. Stay prone—you don't stand up on a boogie board. Go straight toward the beach and enjoy the ride, then head back out.

This time try to position yourself right at the zone where the wave is peeling along—that is, at that point where the smooth, unbroken wave face is making a transition to a breaking whitewater crest. This zone of transition progresses from left to right or vice versa along the beach as the swell makes its oblique approach to the shoaling seafloor. Try to take off and ride right in front of this whitewater, angling along the wave face rather than riding straight in toward the beach. As you ride, the curling lip of the breaking wave might well overtake you, forming a roof over your head. This is called getting *covered up* or getting *barreled.* The overhanging crest might then move beyond you and collapse, or perhaps you'll reemerge from this *green room.* Generally speaking, boogie boarders can much more easily and more consistently get into this special, deep section of a breaking wave than a board rider can. In fact, boogie boarders regularly ride so deep in a breaking wave that they are in a zone virtually out of reach for board riders. It's easy to understand why many people see no reason to use other surf equipment.

The other great thing about boogie boards is that they are not nearly as sensitive to wave conditions as surfboards are. You can ride just about any kind of surf on a boogie board. Sure, clean, glassy conditions are wonderful, but on a rough day of messy surf in a strong onshore wind, the boogie boarders will still be out there having fun when nary a surfboard can be seen. Boogie boarders also exploit sharp, dangerously shallow wave breaks that board surfers simply can't reasonably risk. On the other end of the spectrum, you can give young children boogie boards and send them out over a sandbar with small whitewater waves, and they can ride until they shoot up onto the beach, stranded high and dry when the wave recedes, laughing and giggling, then hop back up and race out to do it again, no other equipment required.

The most important point for you, the aspiring surfer, is that by boogie boarding first (as Wingnut did), you learn the feeling of *catching a wave*; that is, you learn how to position yourself, gauge the oncoming waves, pick the one you want, propel yourself in its direction of travel, and let the wave, in essence, incorporate you into its own energy, shooting you along with it. Catching a wave is the biggest stumbling block for most beginners, and the second biggest stumbling block, popping up to a standing position, is something you avoid entirely on a boogie board. So you can start riding and having fun almost instantly. This doesn't mean that some boogie boarders don't take the sport to extremely high levels, requiring enormous skill, and apply themselves to conditions that at times rival or exceed the most extreme and dangerous conditions of surfing. It's just that getting started is easier, because it's less critical where you are in the wave to successfully catch and ride it, and you don't have to stand up.

Acquiring the Right Gear

Let's get back to our stated purpose now of learning the rudiments and successfully surfing—stand-up surfing—in your first two hours. Pick the right gear and choose the right sandy beach break with the right tide, wind, and wave conditions, and it will happen. You will quickly attain adequate proficiency to start having a ball—you needn't be flashy to ride wave after wave and have a ton of fun. And the more fun you have, the better you will get.

The first step, then, is to acquire the right gear, starting with a longboard, and rather than bore you with endless detail about alternatives, we'll make very specific recommendations. Competing gear and alternative strategies might work just as well, but we know from our own experiences that what we recommend represents one sure-fire path to success.

If you're a boater, you'll know that hull speed is proportional to length. By the same token, a longboard (generally 8' to 11' long and shaped like an elongated oval) accelerates more than a shortboard (generally 5' to 7'6" or so long and shaped like a stretched-out teardrop) in response to the same amount of propulsion. This means that longboards can catch a large variety of waves—small, gentle, mushy—that shortboards may not catch as easily, yet they can catch and perform on big waves too. Further, longboards are much wider, longer, and more buoyant, providing a far more stable and forgiving platform. In sum, longboards are far easier to ride than shortboards, just as boogie boards are at first far easier to ride than any surfboard. You can get a shortboard later.

For now, take a leap of faith and follow the steps in the sidebar "Arming Yourself with the Right Equipment." Wait a minute, you might be think-

Arming Yourself with the Right Equipment

- Go to surftech.com, click "Longboards," click "Robert August," and check out the Robert August 9'6" What I Ride longboard with tri-fins (code 9'6"RAWIR). Go back to the home page, click "Dealers," find the one nearest you, and order one in a color you really like.

- Also purchase from this dealer an FCS or other quality board bag (9'6"), 9-foot leashes (2), an extra set of fins (that's two FCS side fins and one larger middle fin), Rip Curl Bali Split Toe or similar surfing boots (2 pairs), rash guards (polypropylene tops in short or long sleeve that help prevent your chest from getting raw due to contact and rubbing on the board as you paddle—get two), board shorts (2), surfboard wax (Wingnut's all-time favorite is Mr. Zog's Sex Wax [sexwax.com]—get a couple of units to get started, and a bunch of the "warm water" formulation if you're getting started in summer or anywhere it's warm or hot), and one or two wax combs (toothed side for roughing the waxed board surface, back side for removing old wax to start anew).

- Buy a surfing wetsuit matched to your intended home waters and/or your intended surfing destinations. For example, a 3-2 is a good thickness for wintertime subtropical climes such as eastern Australia or southern Florida (the numbers are in millimeters, some areas, like the chest, being thicker than others, like the arms). A 4-3 works in wintertime New Zealand (North Island), northern Florida, and similar areas. Get "steamers" (long sleeve, long leg). We've both had good luck with the fit and durability of wetsuits by O'Neill (oneill.com), but there are a number of quality products out there. If water temperatures don't require it, don't buy a wetsuit yet—board shorts and rash guard are all you need.

- Get sunscreen—zinc cream for all exposed surfaces, and zinc lipstick for your lips. Regular lotions, even the "extreme water-proof" ones, seem to wash off faster in the turbulence of the waves.

- Consider purchasing a surf cap. These come in a variety of colors and styles, they strap on securely, and if you're old and bald like Scott it'll save you. Looking a little goofy certainly beats developing skin cancer, and Wingnut points out that Scott is not going to look good no matter what he does anyway.

- By now you've racked up a significant bill at your chosen dealer, so take your time getting a good fit and making sure everything is to your satisfaction. You should at this point be getting a discount of some sort. Note that your new surfing wetsuit is superior also for diving and any other water sport (Figure 2.3).

ing, are you telling me to drop serious money before I even know whether I'm going to like surfing? Not necessarily—only if your exposure to the sport thus far has convinced you that you should. Otherwise, come as close as you can to our equipment recommendations while renting or borrowing the major items and buying only minor items like sunscreen, wax, wax comb, and so on. If you are teetering on the edge, jump ahead

FIGURE 2.3 The fully equipped surfer.

to the last section of this chapter ("A Further Assignment"), and our prediction is that you could well find yourself reaching for your wallet and hustling to the Internet or the surf shop. Your call.

We have reasons for each recommendation in the sidebar, and we cover these in due course. Nevertheless, a couple of brief justifications are in order before we head for the beach. First, we recommend Surftech boards because they are constructed from epoxy resin on a polystyrene blank and are lighter and stronger than more traditional polyester resin on polyurethane blank boards. Certainly if you live down the street from a custom shaper who uses polyester, it's worth checking out his or her artistry. You'll likely be able to get a custom board for the same cost or significantly less than a Surftech production board, uniquely suited to your size, weight, and ability, and as Robert August recently pointed out to us, that's *your* board, including a custom paint job if you wish. Your shaper will also give you tips, and many shapers offer discount repairs to their own boards. Speaking of discounts, the best deals on used surfboards are almost always to be found among the racks of traditional hand-crafted polyester boards, and your shaper will almost certainly let you take one out for a spin to help you decide.

If you like the strength and lightness of epoxy, just one more word of wisdom on ding repair. Forget the common myth that minor injuries to epoxy boards are more difficult to repair than on polyester boards—the repairs are the same except that you use epoxy resin, which is available from any boat chandler, or, better, in the new kits offered by Surfco Hawaii, Inc. (surfcohawaii.com). More details on repairs in Chapter 8.

When it comes to board wax, you can't beat finding a good brand and sticking to it (no pun intended). Trust us on that one. Wingnut also highly recommends that on that first intimate night with your spanking-new board, before your first outing, or maybe early in the morning while still in your living room, give the board a quick hit of Windex. Spray it on, wipe it down, then let it air-dry. This will cut the polishing compound and let the wax stick better. Now break out your wax and thoroughly rub down the deck of your board (never the bottom) in a tight, circular motion. He calls this "the laying on of wax" and suggests it as a good way to get to know your board. Waxing up the night before or indoors before departure is much easier because you are out of the sun (which will begin melting the wax) and also because your wax will have time to set. You can add a bit more at the beach. These recommendations might seem overly fussy, but having good traction underfoot makes a huge difference, and you'll want every edge you can get. Unless you'd like to go through a Scott-like experience (see Chapter 1), do what the man says.

Finding the Right Conditions and Surf Spot

Time to load the gear and head for the beach—ideally a safe, sandy, gradually sloping beach with little current and few hazards. Bring plenty of drinking water and some fruit and other snacks. You won't have anything to drink the whole time you are out surfing, and while you may feel wet on the outside, you will be getting dehydrated on the inside.

Choosing the right wave is everything in surfing. Simply put, wave conditions depend mostly on local bottom configuration, size of the swells coming in from the open sea, and, crucially, wind direction and velocity. Light or no wind, or a wind blowing directly offshore into the face of the waves, is conducive to excellent surfing. A side wind (a wind blowing along the beach) makes for rough striations on wave faces that may bounce you around and perhaps off your board as you try to ride, and it does not promote ideal wave shape. A hard onshore wind is the worst, blowing onto the backs of the waves, causing them to flatten and crumble, and making the conditions choppy and confused.

Selecting a glassy calm day with significant swell is helpful. Early morning is often best. Pick a lower tide stage, as high tide tends to correlate with waves that build up and then *dump,* all at once, onto the beach. The next trick is to drive along the beach and find a sandbar with waves breaking on it. Look at the pattern of white foam left by the spent breaker. You want to find a spot where the white foam area assumes the shape of a dull triangular tiger shark's tooth, apex pointed offshore, base at the beach. This allows for easier paddling back out for the next ride in the deeper water on either side of the sandbar as well as angled rides on peeling waves (after you get the mechanics down) off the ends of the whitewater sections passing over the middle of the bar (Figure 2.4).

Once you've found the spot, get out of your vehicle, watch for a bit, and make a plan. Which side is working best, rights or lefts (your direction of travel with back to the wave)? Locate the deeper green of the surge channels bordering the sandbar, and get an idea of the easiest paddling path. Lower tide stages are the best for beginners, because the whitewater sections of the breakers tend to be longer and stronger, permitting you to paddle on, make a less-than-rapid pop-up, and still have room to ride for a bit before the wave gives out. Some ideal beginner spots allow a surfer to wade out on the shallow sandbar, actually stand in waist-deep water, pick a wave, turn the board nose to shore, push off in front of the wave, hop on prone, and then stand up as the board surges along on the white foamy section of the already broken wave. This is an ideal way to start.

FIGURE 2.4 Typical triangular-shaped beach sandbar creating a wave break ideal for surfing.

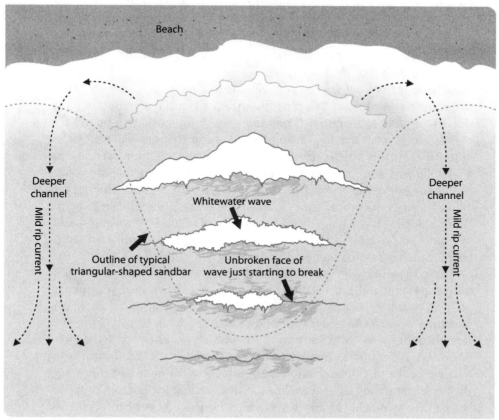

Ariel Medel

Final Preparations

Suit up, remove the board from the bag, and head down to the beach at the base of the sandbar. You or your dealer or shaper has installed the fins using small stainless steel Allen (or grub) screws (if you have an older used board, the fins may be glassed on permanently). Whip out your new box of wax, break the square in half at the seam, and begin rubbing it in a circular motion over the entire top surface of your new board—a last light coat even if you applied a coat at home. Now scratch it up in a cross-hatched pattern with the toothed side of your wax comb.

One more thing before you paddle out: pop-up practice. Aside from catching the wave in the first place, popping up successfully is the next highest barrier for the starting surfer, and it's the only thing you can practice on dry land. Wingnut strongly recommends that you do this as much as you can at home before you even drive out to the beach. It's awkward at first, but if you can do this five to ten times a day for a while prior to your first surf session you will create some muscle memory that will come in very handy! You must balance the board and maintain both side-to-side and fore-and-aft (front and back) trim so that you don't tip over sideways, stall from squatting too far aft, or (the opposite) *stick the nose* (what surfers call *pearling*), like a boat pitchpoling stern over bow in a big following sea. And you must maintain this balance while the board begins surging along on the front of a wave. This may sound difficult, yet going through the proper mechanics first and doing some practicing on the beach will get you popping up in no time on small, gentle waves—and of course you've already chosen a superb learning tool, a full-sized longboard, much easier to pop up on than any other surfboard.

Draw an outline of your board in the firm wet sand near the waves. Lie down on the outline. Paddle a couple of strokes, then raise your upper body on your hands (arms straight, like the top of a push-up). Now thrust one knee forward and under your body. This thrust can be pretty much a straight shot up between your arms and under your chest, or some folks favor a swinging motion in which the foot travels in an arc forward. In either case the final foot position is angled across the board. At this point the knee of the back leg may still be lightly touching the board. Complete the pop-up by quickly rising to a standing position, knees bent, head up and looking forward, arms out for balance. Next, try it again, all in one fluid motion, pushing up with your arms and, using the described protocol, actually hopping up and into position. OK, which foot is back? Most people naturally keep their right leg back, and this is the ankle to which you should attach the Velcro leash strap. If you feel more natural dropping your left leg back, put your leash on the left ankle.

Getting Out: A Primer

Time to paddle out. Watch the incoming waves and pick a lull—an important detail for saving energy. Wade out until you are about waist-deep and it becomes difficult to wade farther. Hold the board at the nose so it is easy to lift over the waves as you progress offshore (for safety reasons, never hold the board in front of you, especially not parallel to the oncoming waves). Now pull your board alongside, pointing offshore, and jump onto it prone.

Adjust your fore-and-aft trim—not too far forward or back—and mentally note your position relative to the board logo. (Scott, for example, puts his nose right at the port-side "A" of "Robert August"). As you encounter waves on the way out, you have five ways of getting past them:

- **Pushing through.** You can paddle straight through a small or weak spilling wave, at the last moment lifting your upper body off the board (see Photo 4.3). With your arms straight, back straight, and one foot raised off the board, let the wave flow past, its top washing over your board and under your chest, encountering only a single foot—far less resistance than if you were lying on the board. Drop back down onto the board and resume paddling.
- **Turn turtle.** Turn upside down and hang onto the *rails* (i.e., the edges) near the nose of the board, pulling it downward, so that the oncoming wave pushes on this slanted shield, forcing you and the forward part of the board downward (see Photo 4.4). Some surfers help this action by nudging the back of the board upward with a foot as well. As the wave passes overhead, push the nose back up toward the surface, slide back down from the nose section a bit, turn the board back over, hop back on, and resume paddling.
- **Duck dive.** This is more or less impossible on longboards, but it's standard procedure for shortboards. You remain right-side up on the board, paddle toward the incoming wave, and just as it arrives you move forward in a crouch and push the nose of the board down, with your lead foot pressing down on the board and the other leg extending aft. In so doing you have pushed yourself and the board underwater and presented a bulky, angled surface to the wave energy, which pushes you and the board down farther. Your arms will be bent, your hands locked either side onto the forward rails of the board, and your body now prone and straight, "flowing" parallel to the board. Now straighten your arms a bit to move your body aft along the board, while pulling the nose up to angle toward the surface. Some surfers help this with a push of the foot or knee on the aft part of the board. Arch your back a bit to follow and ascend, driven by the buoyancy of the board, the air in your lungs, and your wetsuit. You emerge behind the wave crest, safe and sound, having lost very little ground. This technique, executed properly, can work for some very big waves. In Scott's early lessons at Christmas Island, he remarked naïvely to Eric Vogt, "Gee, that little duck dive in front of the wave looks pretty important," to which Eric laughed and replied, "Make no mistake, in some situations your life can depend on it."
- **Cross hang.** What if a big one is coming, you're on your longboard, and you are fairly certain you won't be able to hang on if you turn

turtle? One thing you can do is get off the board, move forward to the nose section, and get an overhand double grip across the deck on the opposite-side rail, thus pulling your upper chest up and over the nearside rail, which is clamped tightly against your midchest (you are effectively crossways to the longitudinal axis of the board). Wingnut calls this a "clam shell grip." You might take the brunt of a good breaker and get washed around and back toward shore, but you and your board will stay together.

~ **Freedive.** This extreme measure violates surfing etiquette and is not an option in crowded conditions, but it is highly effective and quite easy to do. If you are on your longboard and a big wave is coming, the beach is uncrowded, and (critically important so you don't kill someone) no one is anywhere near being directly behind you, you can get off the board and freedive deep, then come up behind the wave after it passes, reel in your board hand over hand via the leash, hop back on, and keep paddling out. It's important to note that this maneuver constitutes *throwing your board,* which is extremely dangerous to anyone behind you and is considered incredibly bad etiquette. That said, if we are trying to get out in a big shore break and no one is behind us, we wouldn't hesitate to do it, and with a longboard it may be the only way to accomplish the task under certain conditions.

If all of that sounds like a little much, don't worry. Remember that you've picked ideal, light, beginner conditions at a lovely little beach sandbar, and if you watch for the telltale ripples of current heading offshore that mark the deeper *gutter* to the side of the sandbar, you can enter at this channel and paddle easily, the current helping you, and you won't encounter any breaking waves in the greater depth of this bottom feature. A gutter or *rip* is to a surfer what a ski lift is to a skier, an effortless return to the take-off point.

Your First Rides

Just offshore of the area where the waves are rising up, curling, and breaking, hold up and wait. Sit on your board and take a breather from the paddle out. You are out beyond the apex of that shark tooth–shaped zone of white foam, which is constantly replenished by repeated breaking waves. Looking shoreward from where you sit, examine the margins of the foam zone—one extending to your left (as you look back to shore) and one extending to the right. These lines define the desired trajectory of your rides, either to the left or to the right (hence the surfing terms *lefts* and *rights,* which assume the rider's back is to the waves). However, you aren't going to worry about getting an angled ride at first. You are going to move in a bit and catch a whitewater wave for a ride directly toward the beach.

Having seen the normal take-off zone, and having marked its position with ranges on shore by lining up objects on land (a palm tree aligned with a section of cliff, a signpost aligned with a window of a house, and so on), and, importantly, having taken a breather and fully recovered from the paddle out, you're ready for the first ride on that beautiful new surfboard. This is it. Pick a lull in the wave sets and paddle straight into the apex of the foam triangle to a position where the waves have fully broken into whitewater by the time they arrive. Wait for the next arriving wave. Line up your board, nose straight at the beach. Start paddling for shore, sweeping the water down the bottom of the board with hand and forearm, alternating arms, forcefully and rhythmically, like a swimmer racing in a freestyle event. Get that board moving! Suddenly the foaming whitewater of the wave arrives, and the board surges forward. Pause briefly to let the board settle into its new trajectory, then pop up to a standing position, just the way you practiced on the beach. Remember, knees bent, head up, arms out for balance. Enjoy it, revel in it, ride it in. You're doing it, for real.

At the end of the ride, or before you go aground, hop off the board. If you teeter and feel like you will fall before this happens, remember that the reason the wave is broken and foaming along is because the water is quite shallow, so don't pitch off headfirst (this is equivalent to diving steeply into the shallow end of a swimming pool). You also don't want to fall in front of your board, or you risk getting hit by the board. Keep yourself safe by falling flat rather than plunging, and cover your head with both arms. Fiberglass surfboards in motion can hurt you, and the fins can slice the heck out of you. Fall away from your board to the side or back, and you will be fine. Respect what that board can do to you, but don't fear it. This is why nearly every surf school starts people on foam boards with plastic fins—and let us say right here that this is a wonderful way to get started. Nevertheless, it makes little sense for most aspiring surfers (with the exception of young children) to purchase foam boards, because they will so quickly be in the market for the speed and performance of a real surfboard.

Remember, this chapter is a formula to jump-start your surfing career. Our purpose here is to demonstrate the possibilities and how accessible this dream is, and we'll save the step-by-step instructions for later chapters.

Beyond Whitewater

Have you ridden several whitewater waves successfully to shore? Great. This time paddle back out to that spot you marked with ranges, beyond the zone where the waves are transforming from solid, building water masses into white-bearded breakers. Sit up on the board, take a breather, and watch exactly where the waves are breaking. Note carefully the area immediately offshore of the patches of foam left behind by breakers. With your 9′6″ longboard, you can start paddling onto an unbroken wave well offshore of this spot, catch the wave, pop up on the unbroken wave face, *bank* the board off to the left or right with slight foot pressure, and skim lightly along in smooth water just ahead of the foaming white section of breaking water. This is the fundamental goal of surfing.

Most new surfers don't accomplish this feat on their first day out, but it's entirely possible in the right conditions. The most common barrier to doing it is physical conditioning. Most starting surfers, even if they're in reasonably good shape, are whipped by the time they've paddled out and done the whitewater surfing—say, riding successfully half a dozen times and falling off about the same number of times, which would be an enormously successful first outing by anyone's standards. They are using new muscle groups in what is great exercise, and their energy is all used up. Let's postulate, though, that you have been swimming laps freestyle to keep in shape, and you've done the whitewater surfing successfully, returned to the beach for some water and fresh fruit, and are up for more.

Hop back out there to the take-off zone. Pick out a pregnant-looking incoming swell, ideally a peak of water that doesn't extend too far to one side or the other, one that is aligned to arrive right to the spot where you are sitting on your board. Decide whether you will take it as a right or as a left. Turn the nose of your board to the beach and start paddling, but not straight for the beach—rather, angle slightly toward your chosen direction, away from the fattest and biggest portion of the swell. As the wave arrives and encounters your board and begins lifting its tail, you'll feel the nose begin to tilt down and the board begin to slide forward as gravity begins to force it *down the hill*. You don't want to wait too long to pop up—in fact, you want to pop up at the first possible moment. If you try it too soon, you will likely stall the board, and the wave will pass you by, but if you wait too long you may get into a steep, difficult, or breaking section of the wave and get pitched off as you try to stand. But this is why you've picked a location with fat, forgiving waves—ideally *spilling waves* (waves that break gradually from the crest and leave large expanses of gently sloped, unbroken water beneath their white foaming tops)—rather than waves that break top to bottom in hollow, massive lips. And it's also why you have selected a forgiving, highly appropriate surfboard that easily catches these friendly waves. Having made these choices, you aren't going to have much trouble. You won't require a perfect, superquick pop-up at exactly the right moment—the conditions around you are a little more forgiving than that. So now you're angling a bit from the direct line for shore, you can feel the board picking up speed, and all you need is a nice, smooth, calm pop-up exactly like you practiced on the beach.

Once standing, knees bent, head up, you have far more control and you are on easy street. A little foot pressure on the inside rail (the edge of the board that is toward the wave) keeps you angled and running along the wave face. You are speeding along, and successive sections of the wave are building up as you encounter them, and you can see the water sucking up into the wave in front of you. The next thing you know, you've shot all the way along and the beach looms in front of you. Increase that foot pressure on the inside rail and the board will bank up and over the wave crest and then you will drop back down to a prone position, ready to paddle back out. At this moment you are finished with your previous life. You'll never be the same. You are hooked; you are a surfer. Congratulations on realizing your dream.

Certainly you have a world of things yet to learn, but you are off to a flying start. Remember that surfing will continue to humble you throughout your life, no matter how good you get, so there's never a reason to let it go to your head.

Where Do You Go from Here?

You don't ever need any board other than that superb Robert August 9'6" (or any one of a number of similar boards by other outstanding shapers). You can take on big waves and small waves, messy waves and clean waves, and have an absolute ball. The steeper and more hollow the waves, however, the more critical it becomes to take off on your longboard far enough ahead of that white plunging wave crest and to get the nose going sideways to the beach at a very early stage in the take-off. Otherwise the wave face bends, the back of your board cranks up, the nose sticks, and you pearl, or pitchpole. Many would argue that shortboards are better suited to these more hollow conditions, permitting comfortable take-offs in steeper parts of a wave and conferring the ability to maneuver all over the wave face as you ride along. Shortboards have pointed noses and greater longitudinal curvature (called *rocker*), which makes them easier to turn and maneuver, but they're also shorter and thinner with less flotation and are less forgiving. Think of it like driving a sports car compared with driving a bus.

Then again, if you've jumped ahead and completed your DVD viewing assignment, you have seen Wingnut and his buddies show time after time that you can ride just about any conditions successfully on a longboard, so why complicate life? Wingnut certainly doesn't.

At a much lower level of accomplishment and skill, Scott in his second adolescence couldn't resist owning a couple of other boards, just for the fun of it. Wanting to diversify, he first went to surftech.com, and under "Shapers" he clicked on "Surftech (which means Randy French)," took one look at the 8′ Hybrid, which is essentially a *funboard*—that is, a hybrid between a longboard and a shortboard—and ended up buying one. Very maneuverable, a great wave catcher, and suitable for more hollow conditions yet highly versatile, this board has given Scott five years of pleasure, and he believes it would do the same for you. (More importantly, two of his pro-level surfing friends, Eric Vogt and Kenny Collette, coincidentally selected and ride this same Surftech board and likewise strongly recommend it.) Unfortunately, Surftech no longer markets this board, so click on "Robert August" and check out the 8′ Hyper Fun Fish, which will do most of the same things for you.

Scott's third board was that 7′5″ *gun,* or large shortboard, mentioned earlier. This custom Bear Board was built by Bill Hamilton, father of world-famous Laird Hamilton, for Eric Vogt, and Eric gave it to Scott, saying it was the next step up. It can take on big reef break waves but is also fun in the smaller stuff. Eric made Scott promise to put it to good use, and Scott kept the promise. Only recently, ten years later, did Scott finally crack it in half. To see Scott's planned replacement for this board, click on "Wayne Lynch," under "Shapers," and check out the 7′6″ Freeform.

Very recently Scott also acquired a 6′8″ Easy Rider (click on "Phil Byrne" under "Shapers") and a 6′6″ Soul Fish (click on "Surftech" under "Shapers"). Of course, you can take your own surfboard acquisition program wherever you wish from here, but the Robert August 9′6″, the Robert August 8′, and the Wayne Lynch 7′6″ should cover you for everything— well, you may want to get that 6′6″ Soul Fish too. As you can see, it can become an obsession.

Lots of folks love to go down to a 6′3″ to 6′10″ board so they can really drill around on the hollow sections of wave faces. These shortboards require a steeper learning curve and more stringent conditions to work well, although the wider, thicker fish designs (like Scott's Surftech 6′6″) are great wave catchers and easy to ride, making a shortboard experience available to older or less skilled surfers. Nonetheless, many times we've been out there getting ride after ride on a longboard when the short-boards (including fish) are struggling to catch a wave and, when they do, are getting very brief rides. Of course, when it's good, these guys put on a real show and have a blast.

The perfect situation is to graduate your kids to a shortboard from a foam learner's longboard, and then watch them revel in the small beach breaks. (Scott's nine-year-old son Ryan started at age three on a 6′6″ foam longboard and now rides a 5′2″ and a custom 5′6″ shortboard and a 7′2″ custom longboard.) By the time they're twelve they can do things on waves you wouldn't believe.

The urge to diversify does not demand that one ride a shortboard or hybrid. In Chapter 4 we'll describe in detail diversification in longboards and their different characteristics. Wingnut surfs an array of longboards depending on the conditions of the day. Still, he always has one very generalized board in his quiver that will be suitable for a wide range of conditions, allowing him to maximize the fun of each and every outing. After all, this is the whole point of the exercise.

Your journey has now begun in earnest. The remainder of the book intends to provide you with immensely valuable information that will enrich and optimize your path. The important thing is to get up and surf-ing as quickly as possible, taking all of the pressure off, so that you can now digest the remainder of the book with a happy smile on your face, tired arms, and salt in your ears.

A Further Assignment

~ Go to robertaugust.com and order the DVDs *Endless Summer II, Endless Summer,* and *Step into Liquid* (also available from Amazon. com, including the option of a package set that includes *Endless Summer Revisited*). An advantage of doing business with Robert August Surfboards is that you can ask ques-tions about anything and get real, competent answers from a highly professional staff, and you can get those DVDs signed if you wish. Watch these three DVDs for the first time in that sequence.

~ After the third movie, view on disc 1 of the two-disc *Step into Liquid* set the chapter "Let's Go Surfing" (surf lessons with Wingnut and Maureen) and the *Surfline* features "The Bill of Rights and Lefts . . . The Final Word on Surfing Etiquette" and "Surfing Glossary A to Z" (you'll want to browse surfline.com too). Then, on disc 2, view the chapter "3-D Fly-Through Satellite Imagery Tour of Surf Locations from Keyhole.com." If this assign-ment doesn't make you begin further frantic preparations for surfing, read no further.

Choosing the Wave

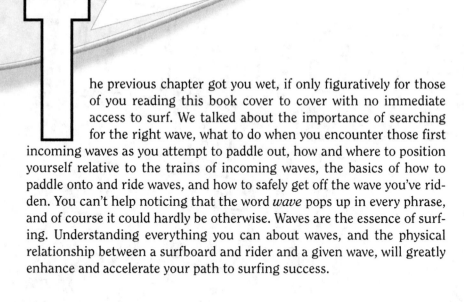

3

The previous chapter got you wet, if only figuratively for those of you reading this book cover to cover with no immediate access to surf. We talked about the importance of searching for the right wave, what to do when you encounter those first incoming waves as you attempt to paddle out, how and where to position yourself relative to the trains of incoming waves, the basics of how to paddle onto and ride waves, and how to safely get off the wave you've ridden. You can't help noticing that the word *wave* pops up in every phrase, and of course it could hardly be otherwise. Waves are the essence of surfing. Understanding everything you can about waves, and the physical relationship between a surfboard and rider and a given wave, will greatly enhance and accelerate your path to surfing success.

The Essence of Surfing

Surfing is one form of riding a vehicle down a slope, analogous in some respects to riding down a mountain on skis or a snowboard, or down a hill on a skateboard, or, for that matter, down a sand dune on a surfboard with its fins removed. Gravity plays a critical role in each case. You point the vehicle downhill, and the hill must be steep enough for gravity to start the vehicle moving downslope. The advisability of attempting a hill of a given size and steepness will depend on the experience, skill, and equipment of the rider. A huge hollow breaking wave is the equivalent of a triple black diamond ski trail. That's why in surfing, as in skiing and snowboarding, we start with longer, fatter boards on the "bunny slopes."

We can only push the analogies with "fixed-hill" riding so far, however. The "hill" we wish to ride with our surfboard is hardly fixed. In fact, it couldn't be much more changeable or dynamic. Sitting on our surfboard in a single spot—a single GPS position on the earth—we might in a matter of minutes experience a flat ocean; then a growing bulge of water as a wave rolls in, building and cresting suddenly to a significant height; then a welter of spray, foam, and rushing water as the wave collapses explosively; and finally a return to a flat ocean, this time with a layer of thick, white foam on top. True, in order to ride this wave we require sufficient slope to get started downhill, but the horizontal push or movement of the wave also has a lot to do with successfully paddling onto and riding it. Once up and riding, like a skier or snowboarder moving down a mountain, we may encounter assorted gradients and characteristics. In our case these form along our pathway as we travel more horizontally than vertically, but like a skier or snowboarder we may choose to cut across these steep sections, rather than speed straight down them, and we may zig and zag a bit to control our trajectory.

Note also that as we ride along the face of this malleable, constantly changing hill of water we call a wave, to a greater or lesser extent water is being sucked from in front of the wave, up into the wave, and then over the top, or crest, of the wave. This flow effectively increases the speed of the surfboard and rider through the water and helps keep the surfboard *planing*—that is, skimming lightly over the surface as opposed to partially submerging and plowing through the water. This facet of surfing is graphically demonstrated at water parks in the form of wave machines, which project a relatively thin sheet of water up and over a steep, fixed slope. (One such machine, Tom Lochtefeld's FlowRider, was patented in 1990 and is now installed at multiple locations worldwide.) Surfers and boogie boarders simply mount their boards at the top of the slope and plane on the flow, riding this artificial standing wave without ever moving downslope—the other end of the spectrum from snowboarding down a mountain (Photo 3.1).

Let's move on to a close examination of this incredibly varied and beautiful phenomenon we call a wave.

PHOTO 3.1 Ryan Bannerot at age eight using a boogie board on a FlowRider.

Photos compliments of Dreamworld, Gold Coast, Australia

Origin and Anatomy of a Wave

Imagine tossing a stone into a glassy, perfectly smooth pond. The ripples emanate outward from the disturbance, the train of longer-wavelength swells traveling out in a set, leaving the faster-dying, shorter-wavelength surface disturbances behind. The bigger the stone, or initial wave-generating event, the bigger the swells, the longer the wavelengths, the greater the energy they contain, and the farther they can travel. Severe storms at sea, such as tropical hurricanes or polar lows, work the same as those stones we threw into the pond. In these cases, the "stone," or wave generator, is wind. These discrete high-wind events generate long-wavelength swells that travel many thousands of miles—perhaps half the circumference of the planet in two weeks—before encountering the shallow water of a reef or landmass. Here the bottom of the swell's circular energy begins to encounter the resistance of the seafloor, causing the wave to slow down and hump up as faster-moving water near the surface overruns and piles onto the decelerating water mass dragging along the bottom. At the climactic moment, the top assumes the form of a tapered shark's tooth. Called the wave crest, it accelerates so far past its own foundation that it dumps over the top, or *breaks*.

The valleys between wave crests are called *troughs,* and the height of a wave is the vertical distance from the trough to the crest, measured from the front side, or face, of the wave. A wave moving in from offshore will normally break when the ratio of wave height to water depth is about 3:4. When the water depth is greater (i.e., when the ratio is smaller than 3:4), the wave won't quite break. If it has already begun breaking over a shallow area but then rolls on into deeper water again, it will cease breaking or *back off,* or *fade out.* This is why you may observe waves breaking parallel to the beach a good distance offshore, then fading out as they progress toward the beach, only to reform and break again closer to shore. This indicates that a sandbar has built up parallel to the beach at some distance offshore. Shoreward of the sandbar the water deepens, then shoals again over another sandbar or the slope of the nearshore shallows. This, by the way, is a common configuration and often permits surfers—particularly longboarders—to catch some fun waves beyond the more crowded beach breaks (Figure 3.1).

Gradual bottom slopes tend to produce fat, broad-based, triangular waves (when viewed in cross section) topped by gentle, small, foaming crests. These *spilling waves* are ideal for beginning surfers. On the other hand, long-wavelength swells that encounter steep seafloor gradients stack up high and abruptly and assume the shape of a recurved fang in cross section, like a mako shark tooth, as the rapidly building crest tapers skyward and then shoots forward en mass from the base. These *plunging*

FIGURE 3.1 Waves in profile. (a) Wave anatomy: *wavelength* is the horizontal distance between successive crests; *wave height* is the vertical distance between trough and crest. (b) Waves encountering a gently sloping, sandy shoreline—wavelength shortens from 1 to 2, wave height increases to 3, and the wave breaks at depth 4, where ratio of wave height to water depth is 3:4. (c) Waves breaking at locations 1 and 2 due to shallow spots (for example, sand deposits or reefs), before breaking at location 3 in the near-shore shallows. These waves are breaking and re-forming twice prior to their final break approaching shore.

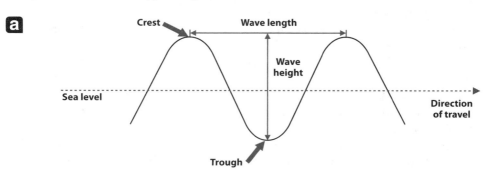

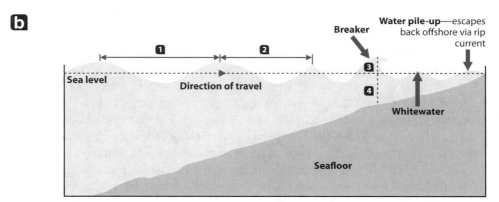

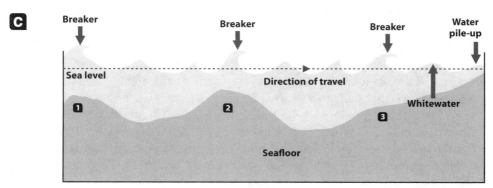

Ariel Medel

waves include the large, hollow waves that form tubes or barrels, spectacular to ride but potentially far more dangerous in their larger sizes than smaller beach breaks or spilling waves. The most famous spot for these is Pipeline, on the North Shore of Oahu, Hawaii.

As mentioned, the standard oceanographic (and surfer's) measure of wave height is the vertical distance from trough to crest measured at the wave face. In Hawaii, Australia, and a few other places, however, local surfers measure wave height from the *back* of a wave instead. This tends to understate wave size, and when you study the profiles of spilling and plunging waves, it becomes apparent that the discrepancy is greater for the latter. The next time you are surfing six-foot waves in Hawaii or Australia and hear locals on the beach talking about three-footers, you'll know why. (Surfers worldwide traditionally measure wave heights in feet.) No one seems to know why surfers in these places measure the wave's back—our guess is that the tradition was born in Hawaii, where some waves are so big and bad that surfers would rather minimize than exaggerate their height. Since surfing was born there, we must acknowledge and indulge this idiosyncrasy, but in this book we'll use the more accurate wave face height to measure size (Figure 3.2).

So what determines the size of a wave? Wind, as we've seen, is the wave generator. The wind's energy is transmitted to the surface of the water through the friction of the moving air mass at the air-water interface. The resulting waves can vary from the tiny ripples of a mere zephyr puffing on a mirror-calm sea to monstrous swells roaring eastward in the latitudes of the 40s and 50s (the Roaring Forties and Furious Fifties) over the unbroken stretches of the Southern Ocean. Some of these swells make their way northeast to classic wave breaks in places like Fiji, Samoa, and the Society Islands. The colossal swells that hit the Pipeline and Waimea Bay in Hawaii travel south-southwest from nasty winter storms in the North Pacific. The size of the swell from any given event is a function of three factors: how hard the wind blows (wind velocity), how long the wind blows (duration), and over what distance of water surface the wind blows (the *fetch*).

Thus, what we know about the wind enables us to predict not only wave size but also wave arrival time. Let's return for a moment to the analogy of a stone disturbing the surface of a calm little pond, and apply it on a much larger scale to a weatherfax chart showing the position and size of winter storms in high-latitude open oceans (Figure 3.3). Each storm will describe an essentially circular area defined at sea level by tightly spaced concentric loops of equal atmospheric pressure called *isobars*. These isobars encircle the low-pressure center of the storm, and atmospheric pressure increases as we move outward in any direction from that center. The more tightly spaced the isobars, the steeper

FIGURE 3.2 Wave types. (a) *Spilling wave*—gently sloping wave face is more forgiving for take-off and riding; note that surf (wave height) measured from the wave back is more conservative than when measured from the wave face. (b) *Plunging wave*—very steep wave face, re-curving and throwing out well beyond vertical as the wave crest transforms into a thin lip, which then extends out and downward as it in turn forms the wave curl, which at its most extreme forms a complete tube or barrel. Note that the surf (wave height) measured from the wave back rather than the face is even more conservative for plunging waves than for spilling waves.

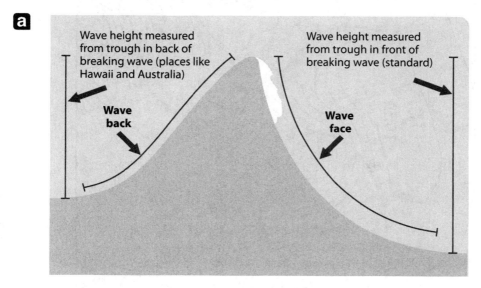

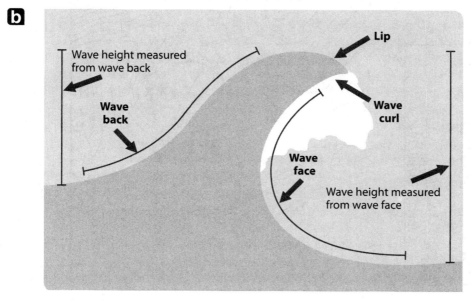

Ariel Medel

CHOOSING THE WAVE

37

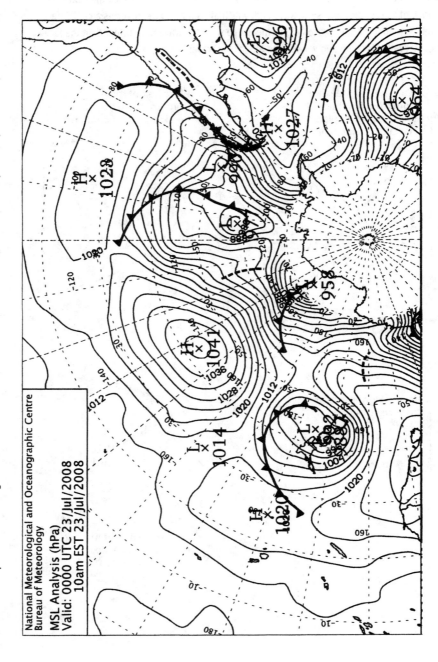

FIGURE 3.3 Large-scale weatherfax showing "pits" (lows, L) and "hills" (highs, H) of atmospheric pressure. Think of these wave-generating events as stones cast in a pond. Note how high-latitude severe weather events send waves to lower latitudes, in this picture, up into the tropical South Pacific Ocean.

the pressure gradient and the stronger the resulting winds will be—much as more tightly spaced contour lines indicate a steeper gradient on a topographic map.

The deep pit of low pressure at the center of the storm system is the figurative stone landing in the pond. How fast the waves will spread and travel from that disturbance can be accurately predicted from the wind strengths in the storm. This allows accurate prediction of the arrival of those long-wavelength storm swells to the beaches and reefs of a distant shoreline, so that surfers can anticipate and plan to be there. For example, let's say it's a North Pacific winter storm and you happen to be hanging out at Christmas Island, Republic of Kiribati, located just 2 degrees (120 nautical miles) north of the equator and approximately 870 nautical miles almost due south of Hawaii. You hear that a big swell has hit the North Shore of Oahu. You know to expect the remnants of that same storm swell to arrive at Christmas just about forty-eight hours later. Those long-wavelength swells travel at twenty-odd knots or so in the open ocean, so that's around fifty hours to go 1,000 nautical miles.

Analyzing a Wave Break

We know that wind creates waves. In Chapter 2 we briefly discussed the major impact local wind has on any given area of breaking waves, and how, in the end of the life of a wave, the part that rivets the attention of surfers, the form of the wave can be enhanced or ruined by local wind direction and speed. We know, too, that no wind or a light offshore wind is ideal; that a crosswind (blowing along the waves) can be tolerable if not too strong and may in fact hold up the face of a wave peeling into its direction; and that a hard onshore wind is the worst because it flattens, suppresses, crumbles, and disrupts waves as they encounter the shallows and break in messy disarray at a given location. Given that wind is a major influence, what other factors come into play in the analysis or choice of a wave break from the standpoint of optimizing a surf outing?

Shoreline configuration, wave refraction, seafloor topography and composition, proximity of passes or rivers, local hydrography (especially prevailing rips and currents), and tides are all very important considerations. Identifying these and predicting their combined influence under prevailing conditions so that you can use them to your best advantage makes or breaks the success of a surfing mission. Let's look at a few scenarios to show you succinctly how to put it all together.

Beach Breaks Revisited

In Figure 2.4 we showed you a typical ideal triangular sandbar, with a swell encountering the offshore apex exactly straight on (wave crests at a 90-degree angle to the main axis of the sandbar). The waves peaked and broke, leaving a triangle of white foam in their wake, the edges of which defined an ideal trajectory for a surf ride. Some beach sandbars are in fact similar to the one in Figure 2.4, but more often they show variations of this basic form. So let's add a bit more complexity to cover a wider range of situations and to demonstrate how to begin reading and taking advantage of longshore and rip currents.

We saw in Figures 3.1b and 3.1c that anytime waves break on a shoreline, the surges of water pile up on the beach or reef or rocks. Gravity then compels these piles of water to wash back downhill and into the sea. We've seen that waves break on shallow bottom features such as sandbars and reefs that are discontinuous along the shore, and that they don't break as much over the deeper areas in between. These deeper areas to either side of a feature like a sandbar or reef thus form natural channels for that pile of water to wash back seaward, and the force of these regular washings scours and reinforces the channels, whether in sand, reef, or rock.

In Figures 2.4 and 3.4b the waves approach the beach at right angles, and the resulting piles of water slide off equally on both sides of the base of the triangular sandbar extending from shore. The channels (also called gutters) extend more or less straight offshore, with the rip current being fed by longshore currents (also called *sweep*) on either side of the channel. An oblique wave approach, as in Figure 3.4a, will yield more continuous, unidirectional longshore currents that feed rip currents mainly from one direction, and the gutter or gutters (with their rip current flow) will extend from shore at an angle rather than straight offshore. In the case of a sandy shoreline, this causes assorted irregular sandbar shapes and breaks punctuated by channels and rips that slant, bend, and snake their way through the shallows to deeper water. This is the most dynamic and changeable bottom type, and it keeps surfers on their toes checking and rechecking along the beach as surf breaks develop, dissipate, and re-form. It also means that new spots are constantly created, affording opportunities for uncrowded surfing.

Longshore and rip currents have other effects on surfing. Remember our discussion in Chapter 2 about using ranges to maintain position in a good *take-off zone* (Figure 2.2), a place where the right-sized waves—ideal for paddling onto—are building up just prior to breaking? When longshore currents or rip currents are consistently flowing over such spots, quickly comprehending these movements and paddling against the

FIGURE 3.4 Longshore and rip currents. (a) Directional longshore and rip currents caused by wave angle. (b) Symmetrical longshore and rip currents associated with wave angle 90 degrees, or straight on, to the beach.

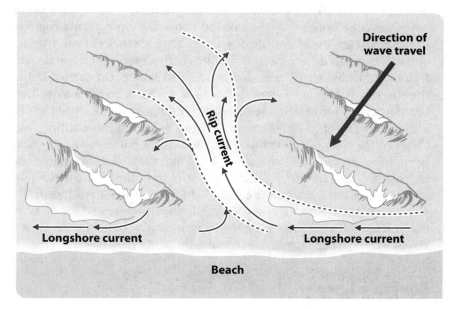

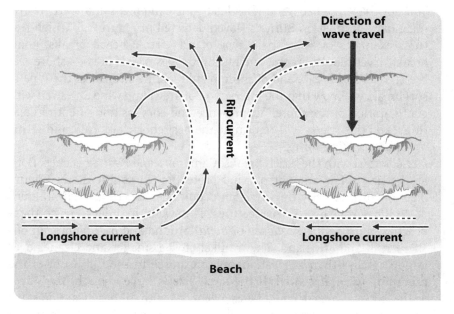

Ariel Medel

flow will result in catching wave after wave, whereas the oblivious surfer who drifts too far off the spots will miss these opportunities.

One of the most difficult aspects for many beginning surfers is to get out through the *wash zone* of breaking waves and whitewater to the unbroken ocean surface of the take-off zone. The rip currents depicted in Figure 3.4 are easily identified by the relative absence of foam (streaks of green through otherwise frothy white surf), surface ripples, and often a plume of turbid water caused by suspended sand being carried out in the current. These rip currents are to surfers what a ski lift is to a snowboarder, a free ride back to the take-off point. It's much easier to identify a rip next to a zone of breakers, paddle out following this pathway, and then exit the river of current to either side. These currents are of course famous for drowning swimmers who drift into them and then panic and try to swim against them, rather than stroking calmly across the flow to areas with less current. Note from Figure 3.4b that often the current pluming off the offshore end of the rip will actually carry you *back* toward the beach, so that if this is where you want to sit and await waves, you actually have to paddle offshore to maintain position.

Surfer's Haven

You now have the background to load your equipment and travel to the imaginary destination Surfer's Haven depicted in Figure 3.5, which features examples of every main type of surf break: beach breaks, point breaks, river mouth breaks, and all three types of reef break—shore reef break, reef pass break, and offshore reef break. Regardless of the type of surf break, we know that the interaction of prevailing wind and swell with configuration of the shoreline, presence and composition of bottom features, and tide stages will determine the best choice of location in terms of suitable surfing waves.

Let's start with the beach breaks, Cameron's and Ryan's beaches. Both are getting a fair amount of wind protection in southeasterly (Figure 3.5a) or northeasterly (Figure 3.5b) conditions, as well as a fair amount of swell blockage by assorted features. The swells, in order to reach these beaches, must refract (*squeeze* or *bend*) around and past points, an offshore reef, and an island. They're likely to be smaller and cleaner over large stretches than at locations more exposed to the full brunt of the prevailing wind and swell. If the swell size is large enough, the waves at these beach breaks could be excellent. As with all beaches, tide stage will have a major impact. At high tide, the water may be so deep that the waves don't break until right at the shore, dumping all at once in unsurfable close-outs—where lengthy sections of wave crest collapse at

FIGURE 3.5 Choosing the wave. (a) Surfer's Haven in a southeasterly condition. (b) Surfer's Haven in a northeasterly condition.

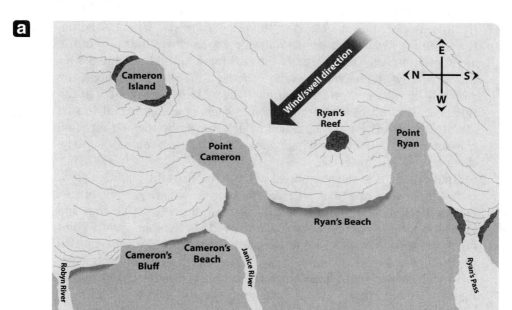

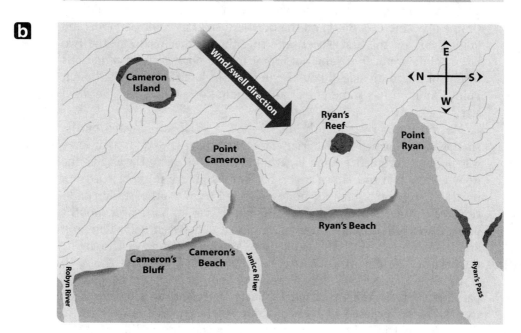

Ariel Medel

the same time. This may also happen on the sandbars at low tide, the water getting so shallow that once more, the waves close out, this time some distance from shore, but still not lending themselves to surfing. On the intermediate tide stages, when the local sea level is falling or rising, the waves may well break sequentially, or *peel*, allowing riders to cruise along in unbroken water ahead of the curl (peek ahead to Figure 3.6 for wave anatomy) and have a ball. Interestingly, at many such locations, the swell will be enhanced on an incoming tide and somewhat reduced as the tide falls. The rest of the specifics about where you might want to surf at Cameron's or Ryan's beaches will be determined by the presence and characteristics of the ever-changing sandbars the week you happen to be there on your surfing safari.

That brings us to the point breaks, which on the right conditions produce the longest, most perfect rides of all of the different kinds of surf breaks. Look at Figure 3.5. Two are very obvious, Point Cameron and Point Ryan, but it would be a mistake to overlook the more subtle point break at Cameron's Bluff. Generally speaking, you find the best waves on the leeward sides of the points (the sides sheltered from the wind) or when a smaller point like Cameron's Bluff is wind-protected, or when light or offshore winds prevail. In addition, of course the swell needs to be sufficiently large to wrap around the point and peel down that protected side. Referring to Figure 3.5, it's obvious that in southeasterly conditions (frame a), Cameron's Bluff and the northern sides of Point Cameron and Point Ryan are the best places, and that the southern sides of the two large points are onshore and not promising. In northeasterly conditions (frame b) the south side of Point Ryan is the pick of the points, although Point Cameron has some potential depending on wind speed and swell size.

Moving on to river mouth breaks—all of which are created by the shallow delta formed by materials dropping out of the water as it loses velocity and turbulence upon entering the sea—Surfer's Haven has the Robyn River and the Janice River, both of which are unprotected from northeasterly conditions but quite protected from southeasterly conditions, the Janice more so than the Robyn. However, both river mouths depend on swells that must refract around and between Point Cameron and Cameron Island, likely requiring a larger incoming swell to create the best surf conditions.

Finally, Surfer's Haven has shore reef breaks at Cameron Island, reef pass breaks at Ryan's Pass, and an offshore reef break at Ryan's Reef. Ryan's Reef is exposed to both of the onshore conditions depicted in Figure 3.5, but in light enough wind and big enough swell it could still be good as the waves refract around and peel down either side of this submerged feature. Cameron Island has similar exposure, yet it is more likely to afford the peeling waves wind protection with its land mass as they refract and break sequentially on the fringing reefs along the shore, provided they are large enough to refract and carry around into the lee of the land mass. Of course, at times of significant swell and either light or offshore winds, either Cameron Island or Ryan's Reef is likely to have epic surfing.

That leaves Ryan's Pass, a typical reef pass break just like those found throughout the tropical Indo-Pacific islands and atolls, a deep, high-current cut through either a reef or adjacent land masses with fringes of reef, affording rights on one side and lefts on the other depending on the angle of arriving swell and, as always, the local direction and speed of the wind. In the conditions depicted in Figure 3.5a, Ryan's Pass is fairly exposed, although depending on the specifics the waves might break nicely enough on the south side to be worthy of trying as a right. Due to the adjacent land mass to the north of Ryan's Pass, it is very well protected in the northeasterly conditions shown in Figure 3.5b, so that if the swells have enough size to refract around Point Ryan and reach the pass, they will be very clean and very nice for surfing, most likely the left-hander off the northern side of the pass.

You should be getting the hang of this now. Although it may seem complicated at first with the new terminology, it is actually quite simple. We are merely abstracting and generalizing a small number of principles to any area of potential breaking waves in the world so that you can choose the right wave. Wind direction and speed, swell size and direction, and features that will refract these swells around them, or other combinations of underwater topography and tide stage, will cause waves to peel. Taking the time to choose the right wave for your experience and equipment is the difference between having a flowing, Wingnut-like experience and one of the many frustrating struggles typical of the prolonged primordial surfing history of Scott.

Wave-Riding Physics

At this point we have acquired the requisite knowledge to choose the wave. This understanding has led us to a place where the wave size, form, shape, and conditions suit our skill level. We are standing there poised at the ocean's edge, and now is an excellent time to focus on the actual forces that will permit us to paddle our board onto one of these waves, feel it surge forward, stand up, and ride the wave. Understanding this will help us succeed. An integral part of this critical sequence, then, becomes identifying the parts of an individual wave and perceiving how these can help us be in the right place at the right time, making it all happen. Peter "Stumpy" Wallace, an outstanding Australian surfer, instructor, international guide, and shaper (stumpysurf.com), once put it to Scott like this: "It's like you're on the platform at a train station. As that train approaches and passes through the station, you want to do the little things necessary to smoothly board and ride that train."

Regardless of the details of wave form, board type, and rider experience, the surfer's goal is to paddle the surfboard as the wave approaches in order to overcome water resistance, which will in turn make it easier for the force of gravity to begin pushing the board down the front "hillside" of the wave as soon as possible, just like that snowboard we mentioned earlier on the mountain slope. In addition to the effect of gravity, the forward energy of the wave will also encounter the resistance of the board and accelerate or push it ahead (this is part of the reason that wider, thicker, and longer boards more easily catch waves, because the forward energy of the wave has more area to work on). Initially, as gravity and the energy of the wave begin to propel the board along with it, the surfer will travel at the same speed as the wave crest, but after popping up and applying foot pressure to bank away from the whitewater, the rider will accelerate well beyond this velocity down and across the wave face (the act of *dropping in*). At this point the downward force of the standing surfer and the upward buoyancy of the surfboard are in perfect balance, resulting in a nearly weightless trajectory downward and along the sloping face of the wall of water. This is the indescribably exhilarating sensation that hooks people on surfing for life.

Picking out the right part of the wave to paddle onto is a very important consideration, and, as you can well imagine, some waves are soft and forgiving, while others are steep, treacherous monsters where the smallest of errors could result in injury or even death. If the rider in Figure 3.6 had taken off any farther to the left in the illustration (behind the wave curl), for example, he could have been projected over the *falls* and into the impact zone. It takes very shallow water to make waves break like the one in Figure 3.6, which means that getting thrown down forcefully or otherwise getting caught in the impact zone can result in making very hard contact with the sea bottom. Sharp coral reef would be the worst, although human bodies can break on smoother rock or hard sand too. Waves at this end of the spectrum are usually the territory of professional-level surfers, and often the motivation for riding the biggest ones is to have attendant photographers get that one incredible photo or video that will make them some serious money. We have one friend who happened to be at Tavarua, Fiji, with a group of pros when an unusually enormous swell arrived at famed Cloud Break (a reef break). It so happened that no photographers were present, and there was no contest, meaning there were no commercial reasons to take the risks. Not a single one of those surfers decided to take on those waves "for the fun of it." We also know many experienced surfers who readily state, despite the fact they've ridden some of the biggest and wildest surf in the world, the absolute most fun they have surfing is in conditions far down the scale from such extremes, relaxed days having fun on quality wave breaks. Wingnut is a perfect example of this philosophy, converting everyday waves into thrilling expressions of art, style, fun, and passion, despite his expertise on the big stuff.

We mentioned earlier that the borderline of the foam patches left by breaking waves defines the fundamental pathway of where you want to ride. The idea is to paddle onto the developing swell and stand up as early

FIGURE 3.6 The components of a wave, and the key forces involved in surfing the wave.

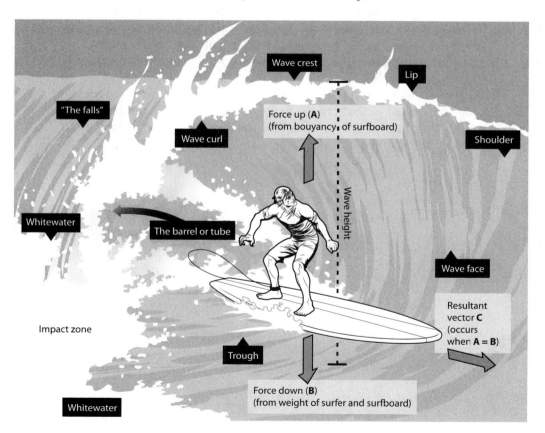

Ariel Medel

as possible, conferring speed and control, and angle down and across the wave face ahead of the wave curl. In later chapters we will describe in detail how to maneuver in such a manner as to maintain this optimal position, either speeding up or slowing down, depending on the wave, doing bottom turns, top turns, and *cutbacks* (turns back toward the wave curl, followed by turning again away from the curl) in order to get back in the best part of the wave face.

Riding a longboard allows you to catch waves earlier and farther away from the steepest parts of the developing wave face, out on the shoulder. As you gain skill you will be able to take off *deeper* and *steeper*—that is, closer to the wave curl. Generally speaking, the shortboard (defined as any board less than three feet more than your height) is better suited to riding bigger, steeper waves and to taking off on the steepest sections of smaller waves. Remember, though, you can ride just about anything on a longboard, as Wingnut proves year after year. You will also notice that throughout the majority of Wingnut's instructional DVDs and movies, he is riding waves that you can ride too. Our goal is to find some thoroughly enjoyable waves that carry no great risks, paddle out, paddle on, pop up, shoot off, and have a fun ride, and then do it all again. Our measure of success is purely fun.

We've gotten our feet wet, we've covered surfing basics, and we are now well-versed in that critical topic of choosing the wave. In the next chapter, it's time to seriously examine in clear, concise detail everything we need to know about the equipment and mechanics of surfing.

Learning to Surf

STRATEGY AND SPECIFICS

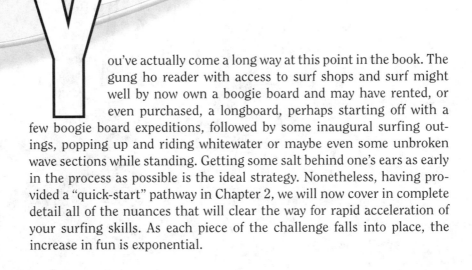

You've actually come a long way at this point in the book. The gung ho reader with access to surf shops and surf might well by now own a boogie board and may have rented, or even purchased, a longboard, perhaps starting off with a few boogie board expeditions, followed by some inaugural surfing outings, popping up and riding whitewater or maybe even some unbroken wave sections while standing. Getting some salt behind one's ears as early in the process as possible is the ideal strategy. Nonetheless, having provided a "quick-start" pathway in Chapter 2, we will now cover in complete detail all of the nuances that will clear the way for rapid acceleration of your surfing skills. As each piece of the challenge falls into place, the increase in fun is exponential.

Equipment Revisited

We recommended in Chapter 2 that any beginning surfer start out on a longboard, and we specifically recommended Surftech's 9′6″ Robert August What I Ride as a prime example of a full-sized, versatile choice suitable for many ages and body weights (as one among many other fine choices of longboards with similar shape and dimensions). Let's use this selection to learn a bit more about what constitutes a perfect board for you, and some tips about surfboard anatomy, terminology, dimensions, and how they apply to you. Then let's look at a high-performance longboard in this same line, Surftech's 9′ Robert August High-Performance Pintail, to demonstrate the effect of dimensions on performance (Photo 4.1 and Figure 4.2).

Figure 4.1 shows the basic body parts of a surfboard and how manufacturers measure various dimensions. This planshape, or outline, is a longboard suitable for a beginning or more advanced surfer. Length, thickness, width at nose, middle, and tail, tail design, total volume, and rocker all affect how the board performs. Generally, longer, thicker, and wider boards paddle faster, catch waves more easily, and are easier to stand up on and ride without falling. Rocker, or the degree of curvature of the bottom of the board viewed from the side, and the shape of the

side edges, or rails, of the board viewed in cross section, have additional influence on how the board paddles and maneuvers in the surf. Now that you've been introduced to the fundamental characteristics, let's take a look at two different surfboards and compare how these affect performance.

The principles we are about to discuss can be applied to any surfboard. Rather than complicate matters at this point by comparing assorted designs of shortboards (which we are not yet ready to ride) with long-boards, we'll do far better to take a look at two different longboards, either of which would be suitable for a first surfboard. Let's look at Figure 4.2, which compares a bigger, more forgiving longboard (the 9'6" What I Ride, or WIR) with a racier, higher-performance design (the 9' High Performance, or HP).

The first thing you'll notice is that these two boards are generally very similar in many ways, which will make the effect of assorted characteristics that differ much more obvious. The WIR is longer and thicker, resulting in 22 percent more volume than the HP, but the nose, middle, and tail widths are proportionally quite similar. The nose of the HP ends up narrower than the tail relative to the WIR, which in combination with the round pin tail design enhances stability and ease of turning at higher speeds. The WIR features significantly more rocker, or bottom curvature, than the HP, which will slow paddling a bit but make it more forgiving as you catch the wave with regard to the chances of burying

FIGURE 4.1 Anatomy of a surfboard.

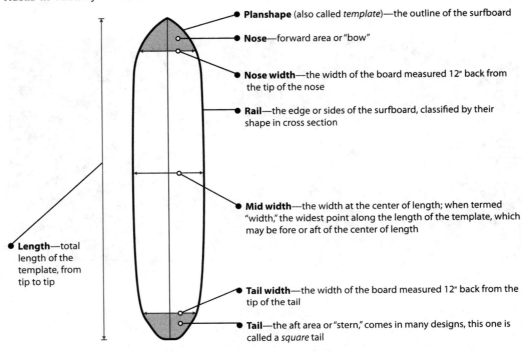

Planshape (also called *template*)—the outline of the surfboard

Nose—forward area or "bow"

Nose width—the width of the board measured 12" back from the tip of the nose

Rail—the edge or sides of the surfboard, classified by their shape in cross section

Mid width—the width at the center of length; when termed "width," the widest point along the length of the template, which may be fore or aft of the center of length

Length—total length of the template, from tip to tip

Tail width—the width of the board measured 12" back from the tip of the tail

Tail—the aft area or "stern," comes in many designs, this one is called a *square* tail

Rocker—the curvature of the bottom of a surfboard, measured at the tips of the nose and tail with board lying on a flat surface (with fins removed)

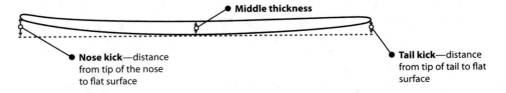

Middle thickness

Nose kick—distance from tip of the nose to flat surface

Tail kick—distance from tip of tail to flat surface

Ariel Medel

the nose and catapulting off the board as it flips tail over nose (pearling). The HP paddles faster with that flatter rocker since it skims over rather than pushes against the water, and for the same reasons also glides more quickly along the wave face. The increased volume of the

FIGURE 4.2 Effect of surfboard characteristics on performance.

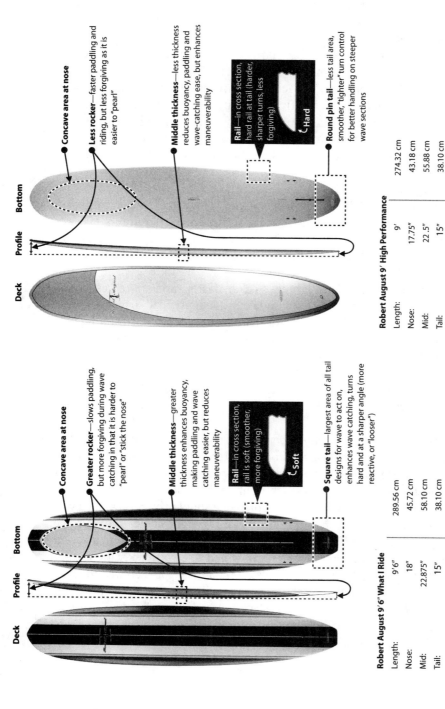

Concave area at nose

Less rocker—faster paddling and riding, but less forgiving as it is easier to "pearl"

Middle thickness—less thickness reduces buoyancy, paddling and wave-catching ease, but enhances maneuverability

Rail—in cross section, hard rail at tail (harder, sharper turns, less forgiving)

Hard

Round pin tail—less tail area, smoother, "tighter" turn control for better handling on steeper wave sections

Bottom   Profile   Deck

Robert August 9' High Performance

Length:	9'	274.32 cm
Nose:	17.75"	43.18 cm
Mid:	22.5"	55.88 cm
Tail:	15"	38.10 cm
Thick:	2.875"	62.9 cc
Volume:	62.9 cc	5.08 cm
Fins:	2 and 1	

(By Surftech)

Concave area at nose

Greater rocker—slows paddling, but more forgiving during wave catching in that it is harder to "pearl" or "stick the nose"

Middle thickness—greater thickness enhances buoyancy, making paddling and wave catching easier, but reduces maneuverability

Rail—in cross section, rail is soft (smoother, more forgiving)

Soft

Square tail—largest area of all tail designs for wave to act on, enhances wave catching, turns hard and at a sharper angle (more reactive, or "looser")

Deck   Profile   Bottom

Robert August 9' 6" What I Ride

Length:	9'6"	289.56 cm
Nose:	18"	45.72 cm
Mid:	22.875"	58.10 cm
Tail:	15"	38.10 cm
Thick:	3"	7.62 cm
Volume:	81.0 cc	
Fins:	2 and 1	

(By Surftech)

Ariel Medel

WIR enhances wave catching and ease of riding but reduces maneuverability in that it doesn't turn as responsively or readily. The square tail compensates for this to some degree, as it maximizes tail area, which contributes to more responsive, harder, and sharper turns, as does the tri-fin arrangement common to both boards. The teardrop-shaped concave areas under the noses of each board are extremely similar and allow each board to plane more lightly and easily with the rider perched over it (*nose riding*), a very useful and fun practice for controlling one's position on the wave face during a ride. The last contrast is the shape of the rails: using hard rails near the tail on the HP helps sharpen the turning ability of this board, whereas the soft rails of the WIR are smoother and more forgiving on the turns.

Basically, the WIR is a larger, more buoyant, more forgiving, easier-riding board that doesn't turn and maneuver quite as fast and responsively as the HP. The WIR is an excellent wave catcher, and its greater length, width, and volume keep it from stalling in softer sections of the wave's trajectory, sometimes making the difference in getting a longer ride. The HP is lighter, sleeker, faster, and more responsive and maneuverable, and in the hands of an experienced driver it can be pushed through much fancier routines in larger and more challenging conditions. Notice that, fundamentally anyway, you could substitute "longboard" for *WIR* and "shortboard" for *HP* in this paragraph and still be accurate, because it's all relative; it's just a matter of degree, and we'll get into much more detail on surfboard design in Chapter 8. In longboard terms, the WIR is the proverbial bus, and the HP is the sports car.

What does all of this mean to you at this point in your surfing life? Well, let's say you're at Surfer's Haven from Chapter 3 and you've used your new-found knowledge to find the perfect waves—small, glassy, peeling breakers. There just happens to be a surf shop right on the beach, and they have both the WIR and the HP on sale today. Which one should you buy? Armed with the knowledge above, you can easily make the right choice for your age, size, and aspirations. The good thing is, both boards are easy to surf and you really can't go wrong regardless of which one you pick. Of course, if you are younger and lighter, say under 100 pounds, you'd do well to forget the 9′6″ WIR and 9′ HP and get a shorter, smaller-volume longboard about three feet longer than your height. Have a close look at the characteristics as demonstrated above and you'll choose well, especially if the shop will let you test drive a similar board from the rental rack.

Getting Out: Everything You Need to Know for Now

Finally, we've not only chosen the perfect waves, but we've also got the perfect longboard tucked under our arm and we're all equipped with board leash, and, as needed or desired, wetsuit, surf cap, sunscreen, and surfing boots, and we've waxed the board's deck. We've been practicing our pop-ups since Chapter 2, and we've been out a few times. Now it's time to get serious about the details.

- **Surf entry.** You're at a sandy beach, you've located a gentle rip current, and you've walked to the base of it carrying your board. Attach your leash to the ankle of your back foot. Pick a lull in the arriving sets of swell—you will reap significant energy savings, savings you can then spend on surfing fun, by understanding the importance of watching the rhythm of the oncoming wave sets and choosing a distinct interlude of much smaller, flatter waves. This is the time to make your move. Walk out into the shallows carrying your board. Note the nearshore zone of turbulent, suspended sand and surface foam from the last wave that broke on the beach. Your first goal is to get beyond that zone. Wade out to waist-deep or so, pulling your board by the nose. Now hop aboard prone and begin paddling strongly offshore, following the ripples of current that mark your rip for fastest transport.
- **Paddling.** Remember the importance of proper trim, not too far forward (which pushes the nose under), not too far back (causing the tail to squat and submerge and the nose to stick up out of the water). Maintain good posture, head up and looking ahead. Use strong, rhythmic strokes, sweeping water down the sides and bottom of the board, causing the board to move along smartly (Photo 4.2).
- **Getting through the wash zone.** While you may be able to get through the white foamy area where waves are breaking (the wash zone), that is, "out the back" to the take-off zone of the surf break (the quiet unbroken area beyond where the waves are breaking) without encountering any breaking waves, odds are that you will have to face some waves. We've already sketched the basics of pushing through, turning turtle, duck diving, cross hanging, and free diving. Let's get some detailed tips from Wingnut now that will ease what can be a significant barrier to the beginning surfer (Photos 4.3 and 4.4).

PHOTO 4.2 Extend your arms fully, then pull back strongly, fingers together, pulling water with hand and forearm back down past you, with follow-through at the end of the stroke. Tip: It's very important to keep your feet together, not splayed and dragging off the sides of the board, something many beginners tend to do because of insecurity about balance. This practice *really* slows you down. Notice how Wingnut not only keeps his feet together but crosses one foot over the other, further reducing resistance to any water washing over the board and adding that much more speed as he paddles.

PHOTO 4.3 Any time you can get away with it (i.e., the wave is sufficiently small and weak), pushing through is the most energy-efficient means of traversing an oncoming wave. Here Wingnut has paddled hard just as the wave arrives, then, at the last moment, pushed up off the board, arms extended, and balanced on one foot to minimize water resistance. This will pop him right over the wave top without losing any significant ground.

Catching the Wave

You know from Chapters 2 and 3 that the biggest keys to catching a wave are choosing the right wave, choosing the right equipment, and positioning yourself wisely and precisely in the correct part of the take-off zone. If you have accomplished those three things, and practiced the mechanics of popping up on your board back at home and on the beach before paddling out, you have made the rest of the process quite easy. You have, to a very large extent, preordained success as defined in this book: having fun doing one of the most delightful things possible on this planet, surfing.

So, you are now sitting there on your board, watching offshore for the next set of waves. You have recovered from paddling out and your breathing has returned to normal (this is an important point because if you are out there gasping for breath and your muscles are burning from lactic acid buildup, your chances of a successful wave capture and pop-up are sharply reduced). Take a deep breath. Study the incoming swells and

PHOTO 4.4 Turning turtle is the "bread and butter" method for longboarders to transit oncoming waves, en route to the take-off zone, that are too powerful to push through. This sequence shows on land what you should be doing in the water. Wingnut paddles strongly, moves forward on the board (a), and leans to one side (b, c), rolling the board over just as the wave arrives (d, e), grasping the forward rails firmly as the wave passes overhead, and then begins to push the nose upward (f, g) to initiate the reverse process of righting the board and getting back on to resume paddling out.

Tip: Turning turtle is also an excellent defensive position if another surfer is barreling down on you as you paddle out and appears not to see you or be able to avoid you.

look, ideally, for fat sections of water that rise to a greater height than the adjacent wave crest. These are called *peaks*. As a peak approaches, notice whether the tallest, fattest part of it will be to your left or to your right, because as you sit back on your board to raise the nose out of the water, and sweep water laterally with your hands to pivot the board toward shore, you want to paddle at a slight angle away from the fattest section, either a bit to your left or a bit to your right, as you are now lying prone and facing the beach. This will shoot you off ahead of the curl on unbroken water, rather than project you into the steep breaking water of the collapsing wave face. So this is the first decision of the wave-catching process, am I going to take it as a left or as a right?

Now paddle strongly out in front of the approaching swell, reducing the resistance of the water on the board by using speed to get more of the board up and out of the water, which in turn will make it that much easier for the board to begin sliding as early as possible down the slope of the swell, and that much easier for the forward energy of the wave to overcome the inertia of the slower-moving board, pushing it up to the same speed as the moving wave. If it's a smaller, weaker wave, even though you've decided to take it as let's say a right, aim the board straight downhill for maximum speed development (just like going down a hill, angle slows the vehicle) and therefore enhanced probability that you'll successfully catch the wave. Remember, this catching the wave is a key hurdle for every beginning surfer, so each and every nuance will assist you. Later, when you are taking off on bigger, steeper waves, you can paddle on at more of an angle, and/or turn more sharply immediately after popping up (the extreme example is taking off on a wave face sufficiently steep that you don't even paddle, you just pivot to face the beach, pop up, and turn hard away from the curl—see *Wingnut's Art of Longboarding* DVDs).

Your next big decision is when to pop up. If you do it too early, the board will stall out, and your heart will sink as the wave travels onward without you on it. If you do it too late, you miss the thrill of dropping in on the most energetic part of the wave face, which provides so much opportunity for setting up the rest of your ride. The key is to pop up as quickly as possible, in one coordinated motion, the moment you feel the board surge forward without further need for continued paddling. Sometimes this happens right away, sometimes you must really paddle hard and stick with it to get yourself over the hump. One trick, if you are paddling hard and feel the wave may slip away from you, is to shift your weight forward on the board just enough to get it sliding downhill, then slide back to proper trim position and pop up. Conversely, if the wave is rapidly steepening on you, quickly shift aft on the board and pop up well aft of your normal trim position, thus keeping the nose from pearling, and get the board turned and away from the curl as quickly as possible.

These little tricks are the difference between a successful ride and either being left behind or wiping out.

Let's get back to that perfect little wave you've found and your nice, controlled wave capture, as illustrated by Wingnut (Photos 4.5–4.11).

PHOTO 4.5 Here Wingnut has paddled onto the perfect stage of a developing wave—a wave that would be just fine for you, too—and he's already made the two most important decisions for successfully catching the wave. First, he's decided to take it, at least initially, as a left, as indicated by the slight angle to his left that he feels the power and steepness of this particular wave will permit. Second, he has felt the board surge forward with the wave, and he knows it's the right moment to pop up. He is already in the first stage of the pop up, arms straight, upper body raised off the board in push-up position, ready to drive that left knee up and under his chest as he hops to his feet.

PHOTO 4.6 In this shot Wingnut has again paddled onto a wave, this time deciding to take it as a right. He has felt the board surge forward and is well into the pop-up, arms straight, body completely off the board and supported only by his hands and the toes of his right foot. He has just started the process of driving his left knee up and under his chest.

PHOTO 4.7 The left knee has nearly completed the necessary degree of forward travel. A split second later, even Wingnut's right, or back, foot will briefly leave or only barely be touching the board as he "hops" lightly to a standing position.

PHOTO 4.8 Up and riding! Pop-up is complete, knees are bent, arms are out for balance, feet are angled across the board with the forward foot offset about 45 degrees to the right of dead ahead, and head is up and looking alertly at the development of the wave. Trim is perfect, with the nose of the board clear of the water and planing nicely on the steepening wave face. Tip: Often beginning surfers pop up to a standing position but look down at their feet or at the nose of the board. They don't see what is coming, robbing themselves of the opportunity to anticipate and maneuver and inevitably ending up in suboptimal positions terminated by falling off the board. Remind yourself to look up, look ahead.

PHOTO 4.9 The next move, oftentimes starting during the pop-up, is to make a turn on the wave. In this case, Wingnut caught the wave and popped up angling to the right, then smoothly hooked around to the left in what is known as a fade turn. He dropped his right foot back and to the left aft section of his board; applied pressure to this foot, which reduced pressure on the nose of the board (notice how it has lifted); tilted or banked the board to begin the turn left; and then began swinging or rotating his upper body smoothly to the left to aid the momentum of the turn, analogous to leaning into a turn on a motorcycle. Note that the mechanics of turning a shortboard are a bit different, in that body rotation really initiates rather than follows weight redistribution (more on this in Chapter 7).

PHOTO 4.10 The desired degree of turn completed, Wingnut now straightens back up on the new angle, but you can see he is still banking the board to the left, holding that left aft rail into the face of the wave with foot pressure, and still has his weight a bit aft, in anticipation of angling across the wave face that is developing to his left.

PHOTO 4.11 Now Wingnut is reestablishing trim following the turn by moving forward a bit on the board, which will cause the board to pick up speed as the tail gets back up further and stops dragging slightly as it did during the turn. If he were to move too far forward, the nose of the board would submerge, or pearl, abruptly slowing or stopping the board and pitching Wingnut off the board. However, you can see that trim is perfect, with the nose skimming nicely just above the water surface. Wingnut is using a technique called *walking* to move forward—notice his right, or back, foot is actually ahead of his left, or forward, foot at this moment. This is a longboard technique. Alternatively, he could have maintained his right foot as the back foot and shuffled forward, which is what happens on shortboards (although the amount of movement is far less). Tip: Maintaining trim is a dynamic process, much more obvious on a longboard than a shortboard with the rider walking or shuffling fore and aft as the trajectory of the ride encounters varying steepness and angles along the wave. Shortboarders do the same thing, but with far less movement, using more subtle weight shifts and foot pressure, often initiated by upper-body movement and position, often with little or no change in foot position.

Popping Up: One More Look

The previous section actually introduced more than just catching a wave, didn't it? We snuck in the whole fluid sequence of paddling on, feeling the board surge forward, popping up, and making your first basic maneuver. Why? Because these first six seconds or less are both the key to and the essence of successful surfing—something surfer's call *making the wave*. Given that you are sufficiently fit to get out there and paddle onto a wave, the most critical aspect about surfing is learning how to pop up—quickly, smoothly, comfortably, and completed by ending up in the correct posture on the correct part of the board.

We've just seen Wingnut do it in the surf in the preceding photos (note that surf movies seldom show the whole wave capture process). Let's break that down from a different angle so we're absolutely certain you master it perfectly (Photos 4.12–4.16). Once you get this, you're well and truly on your way.

PHOTO 4.12 Paddling strongly, head up, feet together, on exactly the right spot on the board for perfect trim.

PHOTO 4.13 The board accelerates and it's time. Raise your upper body by straightening those arms, ending with arms in upper push-up position.

PHOTO 4.14 These two photos capture the most critical part of surfing, that moment when the rider supports all body weight on the arms and hops from a push-up to a standing position in one motion. Wingnut keeps his head up and his rear low. Note that both feet actually leave the surfboard, and that the left (leading) knee drives forward and up and under the left section of his chest. Driving that lead knee is essential—you get that knee up and under, and you've got it made.

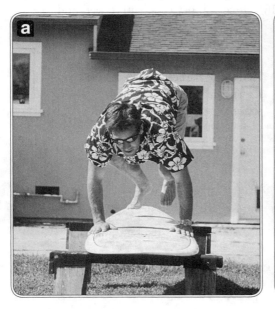 

PHOTO 4.15 OK, he's up, staying low, perfectly positioned fore and aft and side to side on the board. His head is up, looking ahead, with arms just about to leave the board to be splayed out for balance.

PHOTO 4.16 Now he can rise to a more comfortable height in this same basic stance and surf along the wave face. It is entirely possible to stand in about this position and ride calmly all the way until the wave ends up in whitewash or otherwise peters out. You don't have to maneuver. However, the ability to slow down or speed up using trim, and to turn in either direction, confers enormous potential for changing position on the wave face and capitalizing on the myriad opportunities that arise as each unique wave unfolds. And, with clear instructions, it's not hard to do.

Basic Maneuvering

Once more in this section, now that you are smoothly popping up and riding straight, we'll revisit in detail the topics of trim and turning to complete your repertoire of the fundamental skills. In a moment we'll study the mechanics of moving weight fore and aft to change and maintain trim, but first, let's learn how to turn, starting with what is considered to be the easier of the two directions, turning toward the side of your back foot (i.e., to your right if your right foot is back), so your chest is toward the wave face (the *forehand* or *frontside* turn).

On a longboard, there's basically two approaches to executing a turn. The *drop-knee turn* involves moving the back foot aft and to the side of the board you'd like to turn toward, putting some weight on it to initiate and maintain the execution of the turn, closely attended by rotating the upper body into the direction of and leaning into the turn. The other way to turn, called a *flat-foot turn*, is performed less by moving feet around and more by changing the weight distribution with your feet in exactly or about the same position, and matching this with upper-body rotation and leaning at the right time (Photos 4.17–4.20). This latter approach is much more similar to the process of turning a shortboard, whereas the drop-knee turn is distinctly a longboard move. If you moved around like that on a shortboard you'd change the trim so much it wouldn't work—there's just not enough board to be moving your feet around to that degree, and the smaller boards are much more sensitive to subtle weight shifts. Getting back to turn direction, the forehand turn can be more readily executed as a flat-foot turn than the *backhand* or *backside* turn, or a turn away from the side of your back foot (so that your back is now to the wave face).

PHOTO 4.17 Wingnut beginning to execute another effortless forehand turn, in this case a flat-foot turn. His back foot is shifted slightly right and aft, and he is putting considerable weight on this foot, especially on the toes and ball of his foot. He is leaning toward the turn, and since it's a forehand flat-foot turn on a longboard, strong body rotation to the right is really not required.

PHOTO 4.18 The board has responded, nose up, tail down in the water and pivoting off the traction from the fin or fins as it begins swinging to the right.

PHOTO 4.19 After coming around as far as he wishes, Wingnut abruptly reassumes his riding stance, straight up and down on exactly the right spot on the board for perfect trim, knees bent, head up, arms splayed, approximately equal weight on his feet. The board responds right away and tracks straight on the new course, skimming along lightly on plane, ready for the next command from the driver.

PHOTO 4.20 Here's another forehand flat-foot turn by Wingnut, this time in bigger conditions— same technique, just stronger and faster coming down off that larger, more powerful wave.

Regardless of turning style or direction, on a longboard it all boils down to this: you put weight aft and toward the side you wish to turn. You rotate your upper body in that direction, and you lean in that direction. When you've turned as far as you want to turn, say nearly parallel to the wave crest so you are shooting *down the line*, you bring your weight back to center, rotate your upper body back to "lead shoulder straight ahead," and straighten vertically so you are no longer leaning to one side. Flat-foot turning on longboards is similar to doing it on a shortboard, except that on the latter, turns are initiated as much by swinging the arms and upper body as by weight distribution—it's faster, and it doesn't start with leaning the board with weight, as with a longboard. And right now, at any rate, we're concentrating on that lovely new longboard you're riding—we'll talk much more about surfing shortboards in Chapter 7.

That covers your forehand turn. Now let's master the backhand, and you'll be on your way to graduating from a beginning surfer to the ranks of the intermediate surfers. Here again, on your longboard, either a flat-foot turn or a drop-knee turn will work. It takes a bit more effort to turn backhand—you just don't have the same natural lean and leverage that you do on the forehand—so when Wingnut wants to make a fast, hard backhand turn he'll often instigate it forcefully with a drop-knee technique. That said, you can surf for the rest of your life using the flat-foot turn. We'll cover both in great detail so you just can't miss (Photos 4.21–4.25).

PHOTO 4.21 Wingnut was cruising along this wave to his right, and then decided to cut back decisively to his left. He instigates this backhand turn with the drop-knee technique, shifting his back foot aft and to the side of the turn, and rotating his upper body in the direction of the turn. The board is already responding strongly, nose lifting, banking hard to the left. Wingnut is starting to lean into the turn while maintaining perfect balance over the board.

PHOTO 4.22 This photo captures the climactic moment of the backhand turn. The board is ripping around in what for a longboard is a tight arc. Wingnut's upper body is rotated far to the left, and his body is leaning hard to his left, contact with the board supported by the centrifugal force of the turn. He's still in the drop-knee position, keeping the pressure on.

PHOTO 4.23 The hard, forceful part of the turn is complete (see the torn-up whitewater of the back trail), and Wingnut is easing the pressure by bringing his back foot more toward his riding stance, straightening up, and easing the lean. The board becomes more level.

PHOTO 4.24 All of the turn-inducing pressure is off that back foot now, Wingnut's body is no longer leaning, and he is just about fully back to normal riding stance with the board skimming along lightly on the new course.

Once more, it will pay rich dividends to closely examine the mechanics of the backhand turn, the tools you need be able to turn and maneuver happily and creatively on a wave face (Photos 4.26–4.28).

The tendency of a longboarder to use a drop-knee versus a flat-foot turn technique becomes largely a matter of style. The flat-foot turn is a "less is more" approach, like a Jamaican dancing smoothly and rhythmically to reggae. The drop-knee involves more motion and is capable of more quickly instigating a harder longboard turn, especially a backhand turn. Wingnut often blends the two, executing a partial drop-knee to apply pressure at just the right moment during a flat-foot turn. Other masterful longboard surfers do it mostly using a flat-foot technique, as do essentially all shortboarders.

Master your forehand and backhand turn, and do it in the style you find most comfortable and effective. Start small and gentle, and work your way up to stronger, more powerful maneuvers on larger wave faces.

PHOTO 4.25 These last two shots illustrate a very important point about the artistry and flow of a great ride: each basic maneuver flows smoothly into another move. Here Wingnut has come out of that backhand turn, which was a cutback on an unbroken wave face that returned him to the portion of the wave where the crest is breaking (right of frame a), and he uses the momentum from the turn to begin carving another arc, this time to his right (a forehand turn), executed by a simple flat-foot technique, putting more weight on the toes and balls of his feet, subtly easing his upper body in that direction and leaning ever so slightly. By frame b he has changed course 30 degrees or so to the right and is in perfect position at the curl of this wave. What will he do next? Gain speed by going downhill, and use that momentum to turn right and go down and along that wave face we see developing to his right, down the line from the curl. Afterward, he may cut back again to the left to reposition at the curl.

PHOTO 4.26 Backhand turn, drop-knee technique: You are surfing along and decide to turn left (a). Drop your back foot aft on the board and to the side you wish to turn, shift weight back onto this foot, and begin rotating your upper body in the direction of the turn (b). Continue with pressure on this back foot as you rotate your upper body further into the turn (c). Keep that upper body swinging, with the lead shoulder carrying past 90 degrees from dead ahead, and maintain that back foot pressure (d).

PHOTO 4.27 The key to the drop-knee turn is the shift in back foot position and attendant change in stance to support it. Normal riding position places the back foot directly under the back shoulder (a) and approximately 90 degrees to the direction of travel (a, b). Initiating the drop-knee turn demands a significant shift aft and to the side of the turn (c), naturally causing the rider to drop the knee, hence the name of the technique. Note how Wingnut applies the back foot pressure to the ball and toes of the back foot to execute this turn (d).

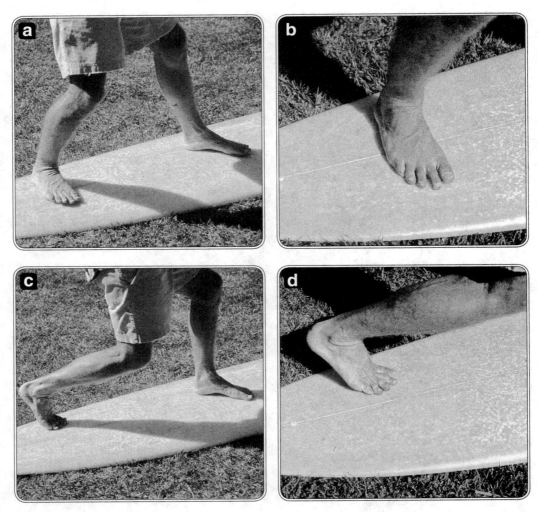

PHOTO 4.28 The flat-foot turn accomplishes the same basic maneuver as the drop-knee turn, but without shifting the back foot. Wingnut simulates surfing along a wave normally (a), decides to turn left, and begins applying weight to the heels of both feet, more to the back foot than the front foot, followed by initial upper-body rotation to the left (b). He increases the amount of weight on the heel of the back foot as he rotates his upper body further left (c), and he maintains this back foot pressure as body rotation peaks just past 90 degrees from dead ahead (d).

Ending Your Ride Safely

Suppose you've mastered everything so far—bought a quality longboard and associated gear, no problem choosing suitable waves and getting out to the take-off zone, paddling on, popping up, and turning forehand and backhand, maintaining optimal position along the ever-changing wave faces. Well, it's a little bit like Huckleberry Finn taking that great ride down the river . . . then what? You're racing along a beach break, the wave softens in a deeper area, then you accelerate as it rebuilds into—you guessed it—a big fat shore dump onto the sand. Question: Do you really want to stay on for this final event? Answer: Of course not. You need to step smoothly off this speeding train and let it continue without you. Doing it stylishly is wonderful. However, the first priority is to do it safely, regardless of how it looks. There are a variety of options, the first of which is merely an extension of making a turn:

~ **Dismount.** You are flying along on the wave, as either a left or a right. Perhaps the wave is petering out as it rolls over a sandbar or encounters a deeper area near the beach. Or perhaps you have traversed a "soft section" and the wave is rebuilding as a prelude to a sudden rebreak right on the sand, called a shore dump. Execute a forehand or backhand turn, but instead of interrupting the turn on a new course or arc designed to stay running along the wave, keep the turn going until the nose of the board is pointing behind the wave crest, applying greater-than-normal back foot pressure to raise the nose up and over, and shoot right over the crest. Drop gracefully to your hands and then prone, the reverse of a pop-up—you could call it a pop-down (Photo 4.29). Paddle back out.

~ **Launch.** Same scenario as above, except this time the wave walls up more steeply ahead, too steep for a controlled dismount by turning the board up and over the wave crest. Turn hard up, or at least along, the wall as before, and when the thinner, curling wave crest projects out over your board, or nearly so, use your momentum to leap free of the board, up and over the wave crest. As with all falls, whether controlled or involuntary (a wipeout), fall flat (horizontal or at a very shallow angle to the water surface), do not plunge, and get away from your board, either well off to the side or behind (not over the front).

~ **Dive.** Same scenario as for the launch, except this time the wave is too big and too steep to turn up and leap off the board and over the wave crest. You are shooting along, and you realize there's no way you can leap over this wave—to attempt it would risk hitting the lip and being thrown bodily over the falls (see Figure 3.6), terminated (per-

PHOTO 4.29 Exaggerating turning mechanics by increasing the weight applied to the back foot, and carrying the turn through an arc past the wave crest, Wingnut gracefully and safely disengages from a wave, popping back down to a prone paddling position, ready to go back out for another one.

haps literally) by being smashed down into the impact zone. What do you do now? Execute a quick, forceful racing dive, flat and hard, right into the lower part of the wave face, entering as close to perpendicular with the line of the wave crest as possible, in order to maximize your penetration through the cross section of the wave. The idea is to shoot through the wave down low, in effect a duck dive without your board, so you don't get sucked up into the falls. You then arc up to the surface, safely behind the wave and well clear of the impact zone beyond. Your board springs back to you tail first via the leash. You grab it, hop on prone, and paddle hard to get away from the area of breaking waves, and out for another ride.

~ **Controlled fall.** This is a rather broad category that includes tame events such as gently hopping off the aft area of your board feetfirst or falling anywhere out and away from the rails or tail of your board (nice and flat, no headfirst plunges—remember, shallow depth is the reason the wave is breaking, and the last thing you want to do is break your neck in "the shallow end of the pool"). On the other end of the spectrum, we have spectacular, life-threatening falls and desperate plunges for the wave base or any area that looks deeper by surfers plummeting off the top of big, hollow breakers after coming unglued from their boards. Be sure to cover your head with your arms and stay away from your board.

~ **Wipeout (uncontrolled fall).** Whether you are teetering around on a small spilling wave on your first day out or expertly dropping down an enormous steep wave face, sometimes suddenly—for any variety of reasons—you get that familiar, special feeling that you are going to fall off your surfboard. The world's best surfers do it, and so do the rest of us. Sometimes it's a wave section suddenly closing out or breaking along too much length—you're riding perfectly, but your glassy hill disintegrates in an explosion of foam. Or, maybe you are pushing to master a turn or maneuver. Perhaps you simply lose your balance. Maybe you mess up your trim, stick the nose of your board into the water, and get pitched off. Possibly you get into a hollow section of a smaller wave and don't bend low enough for the curl to pass over your head, and it hits you in the side of the head instead. Whatever the reason, when you pass that point of no return, use whatever control or leverage you have left to launch free of the board. If you are going over the nose, get low and as much to the side as you can, without plunging deep, and cover your head. Curl up, cover up, keep shallow. If it is a big wave, get a good lungful of air before you submerge, and hang out deep as the wave passes over. Don't panic; don't waste oxygen by struggling. Relax your muscles, stay cool, and then slowly swim back up to the surface after the hold-down pressure of the wave eases.

Maintaining Proper Trim

We've covered the whole ride now, and we have alluded to the importance of keeping your surfboard in perfect trim both while paddling and while riding. As with each important skill, let's dissect and break down this topic in detail so you can master it and use it. Think of a surfboard as a kind of boat. Too much weight on the bow (or front) and the boat will plow heavily through the water and have difficulty getting up on plane. Too much weight astern (on the back) and the stern squats, the bow sticks up in the air, and again it is very difficult or impossible to come up on a plane—that is, get the hull up and skimming lightly on the surface rather than displacing full volume and plowing along. Unequal lateral distribution of weight tilts the vessel to one side or the other, inducing instability and increasing the likelihood of capsize.

We've mentioned that with shortboards, the rider maintains trim mostly by changing weight distribution, usually moving the feet not at all, very little, or by shuffling only slightly fore or aft. This same technique works for longboards, which of course have much more deck space upon which to move around—so much so, that early on accomplished riders began actually cross-walking up and down the centerline of their boards instead of merely shuffling, a technique that developed into an artistic expression and that is very closely intertwined with the art of nose riding.

Many of you will be aware of Wingnut's passion for traditional riding techniques, such as walking and nose riding, and how he incorporates these into his everyday surfing style. Certainly these are good examples of a practical need (maintaining trim) leading to an art form. Let's begin our study of trim at the basic end of this spectrum (Photos 4.30 and 4.31), and then have Wingnut break down his more advanced walking techniques for us in Chapter 7. Here again, longboards are more forgiving than shortboards, and are much easier to learn to keep in trim, because the movements are bigger and the response time is slower.

Regarding trim, just as we pointed out when comparing the flat-foot turn to the drop-knee turn technique, you can surf the rest of your life using only pressure changes on flat feet for turning, and only pressure and the shuffle to maintain trim. Congratulations are in order. You now possess all of the basic tools you need for a lifetime of joy in the waves. Certainly there's much more to add, as you become ready, but it could be argued that most everything from here on out, at least in terms of techniques, is gravy. You've got the meat. We'll return to a detailed discussion of advancing your tools in Chapter 7. Now that you're an early-stage intermediate surfer, however, we need to discuss in the next two chapters surfing etiquette and safety. After all, there's no point in talking about adding to your repertoire without ensuring that you are sufficiently alive and well to use it.

PHOTO 4.30 Often, particularly on slightly steeper wave faces, it pays to pop up aft of perfect riding trim, to prevent pearling and to negotiate the drop-in. The tail drags, slowing the board and maintaining control (a, b). This is also a way of slowing down anywhere during your ride, which has the effect of letting a portion of the wave roll under you so that you elevate back up the wave face, setting yourself up to trim forward and race off at an angle higher in the wave (c) (much more on this in Chapter 7).

PHOTO 4.31 Let's say you've dropped in as described in Photo 4.30, or have purposely gone aft to slow down and set yourself up. Now you shuffle forward—your back foot never crosses in front of your lead foot; it just skips up behind it, and then you skip your lead foot forward, in small increments, until you are as far forward as warranted (a, b). The tail of the board raises, the board accelerates, and you're off (c).

Rules of the Waves

5

The topic of aggressive, excluding behavior by surfers (*localism*) seems to surface quite frequently and quite early in general discussions with folks aspiring to the sport. Everyone seems to have heard about it, and to a greater or lesser extent, they're wary of it. Have you ever seen the movie *White Men Can't Jump*? Whatever else that movie did or didn't do, it very accurately captured the social phenomenon of a "new person" breaking in to established crowds of "locals" accustomed to a ritualistic, recurrent rhythm of participating in a sport (in that movie, basketball). In theory at least, anyone could walk up and play. In practice, it's a little more complicated than that. It depends on the newcomer's skill level, the skill level of the players at the venue, how the newcomer can fit in to the flow of what is already occurring on that particular day, which is related to what may occur daily with an established pool of regular players at this specific location—which in turn will depend on the physical conditions of the area. Each spot will therefore have both a social signature or character and a physical one, and if you can accurately read these, honestly appraise your own skill level, and apply some general ground rules, your pathway to having a great deal of fun will be much smoother.

Certainly it helps if you are a superstar. The pecking order might then instantly reshuffle out of respect for superior skills, particularly if they are accompanied by a humble persona. But being a superstar isn't always enough. Wingnut gives the example of surfing certain spots in Hawaii with a mix of Hawaiians and other local and international surfers. Here, Wingnut describes the pecking order as more purely related to surfing ability, not the fact that you live down the street, have a big mouth and some tattoos, and frequent the spot every day. He says that most of the time the neighborhood crowd doesn't realize who he is, and even if they did, it wouldn't matter anyway. He paddles out, finds a spot to wait well down the line from the top of the order, purposefully picks a suboptimal wave, and then concentrates on surfing it to the absolute best of his ability (which as everyone knows is considerable). He paddles back out, and suddenly all kinds of new doors are open to him. This is like getting an opportunity to join a pickup basketball game at an unfamiliar court, driving the lane after a suboptimal pass, and jumping up and dunking forcefully on the best player out on the court, among players with the grace to recognize your ability.

What about the rest of us? Here's another Hawaii story: a good friend of Scott's, Tom Morkin, purchased a longboard and was trying hard to come up to speed. He lived aboard his sailboat, conveniently docked at Ala Moana Marina, Oahu, the channel leading in to which is a popular summer surf spot. The waves aren't particularly dangerous or overly challenging; nonetheless, it is very popular with a local Hawaiian crowd. Tom is about Scott's age (old—closing in rapidly on fifty), white, not physically formidable, and completes the look with a need to wear professor-like eyeglasses. On this particular day he paddled out to the take-off zone and kind of waited around as a couple of the big, muscular locals got wave after wave. Finally a little peak came along his way, he paddled on, and just as he wobbled up to a standing position, a very large, brown, heavily tattooed Hawaiian loomed up from his left, and Tom immediately lost his balance and fell. The local swung aside gracefully and dismounted, and, very close to Tom, asked loudly, *"What're you doing, bro?"* At this point, Tom was frozen, and he said he was thinking he might not survive whatever was coming next. He was stammering out an apology, when the Hawaiian exclaimed forcefully, "Get on your board and get over here, bro. You can't take off over there. You come sit right over here with me, and we're going to get you on a wave." Tom, trying not to weep in relief, gratefully followed and had a great afternoon.

This chapter will give you all the information you need to maximize your surfing fun by understanding what is going on around you and following established etiquette. This starts with "rules of the road," not unlike the international collision-avoidance regulations one must pass for maritime vessel operating licenses, and continues with the social mores and ethics of surfing.

More Surf Stories

To begin, let's not sugarcoat the topic of surf aggression too much. The superstars don't always get exposed to normal-person surf experiences. Let's get a few somewhat more extreme stories out of the way, for perspective, and then go over exactly what you need to know to never have any trouble. Years ago Scott was asking Eric Vogt about a scene from *Endless Summer II* where a surfer comes shooting out of a barrel and runs over the legs of another surfer who was paddling out right across his pathway. The guy coming out of the barrel couldn't have avoided it. Surfboard fins are quite sharp and can cut quickly and deeply, and if you look at that scene, the paddler would almost certainly have been slashed deeply across the back of his calves. Eric commented that this happens sometimes, and basically it is the fault of the person paddling out into the wrong area.

He went on to describe a similar event, shooting out of a barrel while surfing a very big day at his home break at Kauai, Hawaii, and running over another surfer paddling out—no time to turn or avoid. (Eric did say that at some breaks there were locals who would try to run over other surfers "invading their turf," going so far as to jump on their boards as they traversed the body of the hapless paddler, not something he would ever do.) When he paddled back out to the take-off zone, the guy he'd run over, a muscular young fellow, and his older brother stroked quickly over to Eric and began screaming at him. Eric, like Tom, isn't imposing looking. Unlike Tom, Eric has a black belt in tae kwon do. Eric waited silently for them to slow down, and then interjected in a soft voice, "Listen, I didn't mean to run over you. You need to be much more careful about where you paddle out. As far as what happened, even though I couldn't possibly have avoided it, you have my apology. Now, that said, it's time for you both to either shut up or give me your worst." The two fellows paused for a moment to digest Eric's words, looked at each other, and quietly paddled away.

There is the odd punch-up or loud confrontation in some places, and sometimes an angry surfer will wait on the beach for a combatant to paddle in, and continue the affair on land. In Australia, for example, places along the Gold Coast and Sydney-area surf beaches have bad reputations for aggressive behavior that violates surfing etiquette and worse. Other areas, particularly where crowds compete for good surf, have similar problems. Once in California, another friend of Scott's, named Robert, also a martial artist and an expert surfer (and another "old man"), described attempting to mind his own business at a surf break only to be harassed quite unreasonably. Again, the culprits were two very fit, large younger men who were brothers. They followed him all the way to the parking lot, becoming more and more aggressive. Finally, as Robert tried to get in his car, the larger of the two launched himself at Robert, who calmly dropped him with a fast sequence of precision blows, shattering his nose. The fallen young assailant, on his knees, began sobbing inconsolably, and his brother abruptly decided to become more conciliatory. Robert calmly counseled, "You need to think about treating other people with more respect. Share more, be nice, and things will go better for you, and you'll be a happier person. Learn from this lesson," and then drove away.

OK, that's it for the rough stuff. You couldn't get more average or regular than Scott, and although his surfing history is mostly in Australia, New Zealand, and scattered Pacific islands, he's never had any significant trouble in hundreds of outings, and never personally witnessed a single act of surf-related violence. Wingnut has a much broader perspective, many more outings, and he's never had anything violent happen to him either. And neither will you. Pick your spots, relax, smile, and if you do end up sharing a place with other surfers, know the rules, show some respect while standing your ground, and you will be fine. We'll also give you some very effective tips for space- and opportunity-sharing in the surf.

Surfing Sociology

No one owns waves. As you read this, thousands of beautiful waves are breaking all over the planet, glittering in the sun, and no human eyes are seeing them. Imagine slicing along smartly into a pass through the reef of an uninhabited tropical atoll, far out in the Pacific Ocean, at the helm of your own sailboat, a quiver of surfboards lashed neatly to the rail, gazing at lovely curling breakers at the mouth. The only locals have fins. You and your crew mates will be the only ones there.

Most of us, however, will far more often be surfing at places where we aren't the first, and seldom the only, surfer in the water. Consistently good surf attracts people. Some find ways to live nearby. Inevitably, they are frequently out there on their boards . . . just like you. In Chapter 3 we covered in great detail how to choose your surf spot based on physical parameters. Now we need to learn how to read the sociological parameters of a surf spot and how they relate to you.

The first step derives directly from your assessment of the waves. Some spots regularly feature beginner waves, others intermediate or advanced waves. An ideal beginner spot might have a gradually sloping sand bottom, relative protection from the extremes of wind and swell, with small, well-formed spilling waves breaking sequentially and gently along the beach at the right tide. Beginners and less experienced surfers will flock to this place. Another spot might frequently feature huge, hollow plunging waves that suck up off a treacherously sharp, shallow rock or coral shelf, roaring across a reef corner and into a high-current, deep pass patrolled by large predators. Conditions at this end of the spectrum warrant a figurative huge red neon sign flashing "Experts with a Death Wish Only." The typical crowd here will be just that.

Most places are in between. Where do you fit? What kind of equipment do you have? Are you capable of riding what's out there today? How many surfers are out? When a wave rolls in, how many surfers are attempting to take off on it? Are they spread out or clustered? Do you have the maneuvering skills to negotiate the crowd? What's the general appearance of the crowd? Moms, pops, and kids on longboards, or ex-convict gangster types jostling for position on shortboards? Generally, the less crowded, the more laid-back, and the greater the variety of surfboards present, the easier-going the social conditions will be. Is there another break nearby that is surfable but has fewer or no surfers on it?

If it's not too crowded for your tastes and you can honestly say you have a good chance of handling the waves, paddle out and see what it's like. Don't shy away even if the conditions are a step up for you. You can always stay off to the side and observe. You will quickly get a feel for the skill and temperament of the location by listening, sizing up the demography of who's out, and watching how this changes over time. You can sit outside or in a more marginal take-off zone, and the occasional wave will sneak through so you can have it all to yourself. Take it slowly. Try different spots. You will quickly grasp which ones are right for you. Wingnut, for example, regularly surfs only five or six local breaks near his California home, and he surfs five or six times a week. This is often enough to be a regular feature at these spots and to retain his position in the pecking order—or at least be recognized as a regular and not have to go through the whole process of establishing himself in the lineup again. Scott is fortunate to live near a long stretch of beach in eastern Australia with changeable sandbars, spreading out and minimizing the number of surfers much of the time, with three point breaks nearby, equating roughly to the frequency that Wingnut shows up at his spots. There aren't as many people, so no real pecking order exists, except on the big days among the expert riders who establish themselves in the lineup during any particular time span. Some days and some places can get quite crowded, but Scott uses the little routines he learned from Wingnut to minimize the effect on surfing fun, the same ones we're about to go over with you.

Rules of the Road

Before we learn how to "beat the crowd," it is essential to understand and adhere to the basic rules of surfing etiquette and custom:

~ **Never paddle out through a take-off zone or riding path.** Try your best to avoid influencing the ride of fellow surfers when you are paddling out by avoiding the area where rides are frequently crossing through, or where surfers are paddling on and popping up. If you wipe out early, you may not be able to help but paddle through such an area, and this may place you in someone's path. In this case paddle hard for their inside, into broken whitewater, so they can ride the unbroken wave face without having to avoid you. This may be a bit tougher on you, but it's only fair to them. If a rider doesn't see you and it looks like he or she will run over you, turn turtle or free dive deep without your board to avoid injury. If you make eye contact with the oncoming surfer, and you know the person has the skills and is willing to avoid you, sit still rather than making a last-minute surge he or she may not expect. When this happens, it never hurts to thank the surfer when he or she comes back out to the lineup and apologize if you messed up the person's ride. Be equally avoidant and gracious if you are on the other end of the situation. It's much better to purposely terminate a ride than to hit another surfer.

~ **Inside position has the right of way.** The surfer closest to the curl is termed *inside*. For example, imagine paddling onto a right-hand wave at a point break. Several other surfers are also paddling onto the wave. You feel the board surge and you think you can make it. You look to the left (inside) and see another surfer surging and starting the pop-up, closer than you are to the breaking whitewater. You should push yourself back on your board, spread your legs off either rail, and pull the nose up to stall, giving way to this surfer. If, on the other hand, you glance left and no one is there, or the surfer isn't going to catch the wave (at which time a respectful fellow surfer will yell out to you to take it or go for it), keep stroking hard, pop up, and ride . . . but as you do, look over to your right to check for someone who may be *dropping in* on you (taking off outside of you out of turn, inadvertently or otherwise). If so, it's better to give way either by surfing straight or by stalling than to have a collision. If you are up and riding and this begins to happen, a polite but loud "inside" or "hey" will normally assist the other surfer's decision to lay off (that is, purposely stall) or at least turn sharply and dismount to get out of your way. No matter how careful and respectful you and other surfers are, accidental drop-ins will occur from time to time. If you do it, try to turn hard and get off the wave. As the surfer whose ride you may have messed up paddles back out, take the trouble to apologize, letting him or her know you understand proper etiquette and you didn't do it intentionally. If it happens the other way around, be graceful and forgiving, and above all, avoid collisions. Humility and respect are powerful inducements for eliciting similar behavior out of other surfers. Treat others how you would like to be treated and it will come back to you.

~ **Take turns; do not snake.** The term *snaking* refers to surfers who either are just paddling out to the lineup of surfers in the take-off zone or are sitting outside the inner take-off positions but closer to shore and quickly paddle to an inside position and take off "inside," thereby claiming the wave. In other words, they don't wait their turn in any sort of manner; they "snake" to jump the queue. Another way these kind of people may do this is to paddle out, ignore the waiting order of surfers, and position all the way inside, despite having just had a ride. This is an abuse of the fundamental inside right-of-way rule and is not the kind of behavior that will establish a positive rapport with others, at the very least. Watch how the other surfers are working—the highly skilled among them will be taking off deep and steep, sometimes so much so that they get closed out from their attempt to claim the wave. The pecking order extends out from here. If you have stood by while others get turns, and it's your turn, and you can handle it, get right in there and claim your wave. Note that generally, if you go for a wave, even if you miss it or wipe out, that was your turn, and you go to the end of the line.

~ **Up and riding has right of way.** Generally, if you have popped up and you are riding the wave, regardless of position, you have rightfully claimed the wave. However, unlike the inside position rule, this rule is more flexible. For example, let's say you paddle out on an 8′ hybrid surfboard to a point break, and the other surfers are skilled and on much shorter high-performance boards (all well under 7′). You paddle out beyond the crowd, because the greater hull speed of your board allows you to catch the wave at an earlier, less steep (*critical*) stage. A beautiful swell rolls in; you catch it, pop up, and come racing in through the lineup. You have the right of way; it's your wave. If you then do it again, as soon as you get back out, and before others have had a shot, you would be pushing the code of taking your turn. Wingnut would say you've probably gone a bit further, angering the entire pecking order with a challenge to the established situation. Now, let's say you sit outside and slightly beyond the inner take-off points. A swell comes in, you catch it and pop up, but one of the skilled surfers is taking off well inside you deep and steep. He or she comes racing out along the wave face, and you're already there. This person will likely think you dropped in and he or she has the right of way. This is a gray area, and no matter the details of the timing, given all the circumstances, you will likely need to give way, even though technically you could argue you had the right of way. So, although *up and riding* does have the right of way, *inside position* is the stronger rule of the road and may sometimes take precedence, all things considered. Another thing that doesn't really work is when someone catches a wave in the normal take-off zone, and then another rider further in catches the wave well back in the whitewater and begins working out toward the surfer on the unbroken wave face. Technically, the inside-out rule applies, yet you can be sure that even if the other surfer in the outside position yields it will be begrudgingly. Exercising the inside position rule in this situation is not a good idea.

Figure 5.1 illustrates practical application of surfing rules of the road for Surfers 1, 2, 3, and 4. Surfer 1 is the farthest inside but is still prone. Surfer 2 is next out but up and riding before Surfer 1 has popped up. If 1 and 2 had taken off from nearly side by side and they pop up anywhere close to the same time, 2 should give way (unless 1 has snaked). However, if 2 is well up and riding, having paddled on well before 1, 2 should have the right of way—particularly if 1 started closer to the bottom of the figure and inside, having just arrived, meaning 1 is snaking 2. Surfer 3 is both outside and still just popping up and needs to immediately give way to 2. Surfer 4, under the circumstances, has no business trying for this wave and should immediately stall and pull off. This snapshot would seem to indicate this wave belongs to Surfer 2. What if 1, 2, 3, and 4 are all buddies and 1 or 2 yells out "Party wave!"? Then all four surfers should paddle on, pop up, and ride together, taking care to keep relatively straight so as not to collide with one another.

Surfing Ethics

We've established the harder, faster rules of surfing, and we have already seen how the loopholes or gray areas can loom up and create opportunities for abuse. One of the main forms of such abuse can be using specific characteristics of surfing equipment to bully other surfers, for example, to run roughshod over the concept of taking turns. The classic example is that longboards catch waves more easily and earlier in their development than shortboards. A point break frequented by longboarders can therefore be very difficult for a shortboarder to get very many waves, especially if it's crowded. In this case, the surfers nearest the shortboarder can be diplomatic by throwing the person a few bones. Most likely the best thing is for the shortboarder to find a surf break with more shortboarders.

The same sort of thing can happen between boogie boarders and surfers of any flavor. Boogie boarders can take off shallower and steeper than surfboard riders, which often translates into inside position. If they repeatedly claim waves starting inside a less steep, deeper area where surfers are taking off, this could prevent a group of surfers from catching the waves. While boogie boards are smaller and softer than surfboards, allowing more risk-free opportunities for wave-sharing among them, if a

FIGURE 5.1 Who has the right of way?

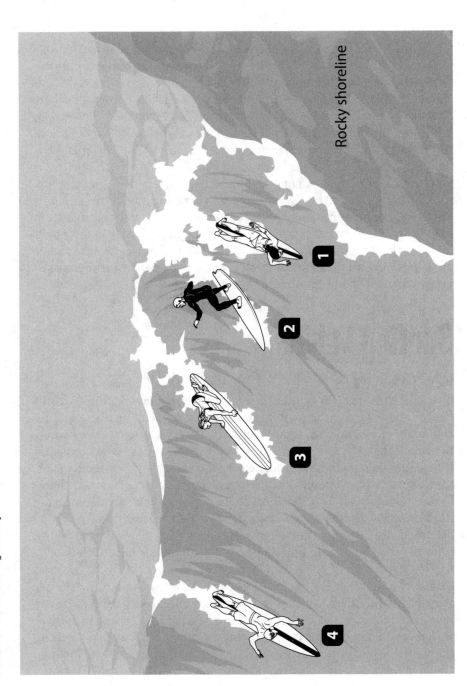

Rocky shoreline

Ariel Medel

surfer drops in on or otherwise runs over a boogie boarder, serious injury can result. Maybe that's why it can be generally said that boogie boarders tend to be quite good about waiting their turn in mixed-equipment surf breaks. Of course, they also surf many spots over shallow rocks, and in deep, hollow shore breaks that would be practically impossible for a surfboard rider to attempt.

Now let's return to that point break with all of the longboarders. What if a group of stand-up paddle (SUP) surfers come out? SUP boards are generally longer and fatter than longboards, and the rider is standing up stroking with a powerful paddle. Guess what? These surfers can catch waves at an even earlier stage than the longboarders, just as can most surf skis, outrigger canoes, and kayaks. And the tow-in guys behind Jet Skis can outrace and outcatch any of the above, while projecting a big wake that sends disruptive wavelets over the faces of swells rolling in to the paddle-on surfers.

The solution is obvious: a little respect, common sense, and consideration for others goes a long way. It's all good fun. Different locations and different day-to-day conditions lend themselves to different gear and to different skill levels within any gear category. Wingnut loves to SUP surf on days too small to surf conventionally, and he boogie-boarded almost exclusively, remember, until the age of sixteen. Scott and his son Ryan sometimes leave the surfboards at home and take boogie boards out to shallow reef and rock breaks that would tear the fins and bottoms right out of the boards, and they have an absolute ball. Be aware of the specific advantages of your equipment relative to those around you, and don't use these to take an unfair proportion of the incoming waves.

Mitigation and Strategy

We've been over the topic of ascertaining both the physical and social signature of a surf spot, and we know the rules of the road and the fundamentals of surfing etiquette. How can we use aspects of surf sociology and oceanography to maximize our experience? Here are a few secrets that really work.

- **Taking advantage of the "witness relocation program."** One very pronounced tendency of surfers is to bunch up on one specific break and compete for what they feel is the "best" wave. Let's say you arrive at the beach, pick out a sandbar, paddle out alone, and start catching a few rides. If there's anyone about, you will be surprised how quickly you have company. It's just like fishing an area with other boats around: when your rods start to bend, you'll soon have plenty of new friends. Wingnut calls this sheeplike mentality the "witness relocation program." Here's how to mitigate it. When you get to the beach, you will likely see surfers bunched up on one or two of say half a dozen sandbars. Wingnut will watch for a bit, pick out three or four specific take-off zones in advance, and then paddle out to one with few or no surfers on it. He'll catch a few good rides, drawing a crowd. Then he'll move over to the next spot—which may well be the one they've just abandoned—catch a few more waves, then when the pack arrives, paddle to the third spot, get a few rides . . . and so on. Shifting and rotating like this keeps you riding in relatively uncrowded conditions even with a fair number of surfers out.

~ **Wave-sharing.** More relaxed surf spots, featuring a wider variety of ages and a significant proportion of longboarders, will often permit wave-sharing—that is, a relaxation, to some degree, of the inside position rule for laying sole claim to a wave. One way this may occur is if you catch a wave and encounter another surfer attempting to paddle on, or perhaps already dropped in and riding to your outside. Rather than calling them off, you can *call them on*. Tell them to stay on or join you. Especially if this is a young beginning surfer or an older surfer who has been struggling to get a wave, you will have just made a new friend. Another way this may occur is if you have been doing well getting rides, and you notice another surfer struggling. The next time you paddle out, tell the person not to lay off any wave you may have and feel free to join in. This likely won't cost you much anyway, since the surfer has already established that he or she is not likely to catch most waves, and if he or she does get one that causes you to have to go straight instead of along the wave face, so what? You've done a good deed.

~ **Party waves.** Groups of neighborhood kids surfing a relaxed location will sometimes yell out "Party wave!" and everyone—sometimes seven or eight at a time—paddles on and rides straight, laughing and talking the whole way.

~ **Board-sharing.** Yet another way to help someone you see who is having a hard time may be to give the person a few rides on your board. Scott has done this on a number of occasions on small days at longboard spots with his Robert August 9′6″ WIR and a couple of times with his Randy French 8′ Hybrid, especially with kids. One very early morning, for example, he was surfing the same sandbar as a twelve-year-old named Harry who had a very beat-up, waterlogged old shortboard and just couldn't seem to get a wave. On the Hybrid, the young fellow took off on the first swell like greased lightning and had a wonderful ride screaming all the way down the line, popping off just before the shallows. His face lit up like a Christmas tree. He had to go to school in a half hour, so Scott just let him ride it the whole rest of his time. On every occasion since, when Harry and his friends see Scott, they treat him like a revered uncle (and Harry quickly thereafter acquired a new board). Several other fast surfing friendships, with a variety of ages and genders, have been born in the same manner. Like this book, the motivation is to ease the path for others. And on several occasions, it's actually been the reverse, swapping boards just for fun with surfers who turn out to be experts, and getting all kinds of insights and tips in return.

~ **Peak-sharing.** Oftentimes an incoming peak, let's say to the apex of a sandbar, can be ridden by two surfers equally with absolutely no interference if one surfer takes it as a right and another takes it as a left. Even if you don't know the fellow surfer, you can always inquire "going right?" or "going left?" and it will be understood that you are going to take the opposite. This then clears two riders from the lineup and makes the next swell available to others.

~ **Creative pathways.** A slightly more complex strategy that works well in crowds, including more competitive surf spots, is to have a good look at the way the pack is distributing, and analyze the question "Is there a more creative pathway?" Figure 5.2 illustrates just one example, and this is a real case: consider a point break that features two main take-off zones, the most popular of which (A) leads to a long, strong right-hander. There are more than twenty longboarders loaded up on that right, competing for the take-off at wave stage (WS) 1, like Surfer R. However, the wave is actually a peak with a short left-hand ride available, and then the entire wave fades as it encounters a deeper zone, only to reform and break again similarly further along. The main pack takes the strong right, then the riders dismount on that first fade to paddle back to the take-off point (as per Surfer R, WS 1 through 5). Another smaller group of surfers is sitting on the right-hander take-off point (B) for the rebreak. You know what works perfectly? Sitting well to the side of, but even with, the outer pack at A, at your own take-off zone (L) taking the peaks initially as a left (as per WS 1, Surfer L), and then as the left-hander fades, cutting back, all the way across and in front of the shrinking whitewater (see the move of Surfer L, WS 4 and 5) still on unbroken wave face, catching the right-hander as it re-forms (WS 6), and riding that all the way (WS 7 to 10). There's no competition for that left-hand take-off (L), because all the other surfers are bunched up on the right-hand take-off (A). Regarding the

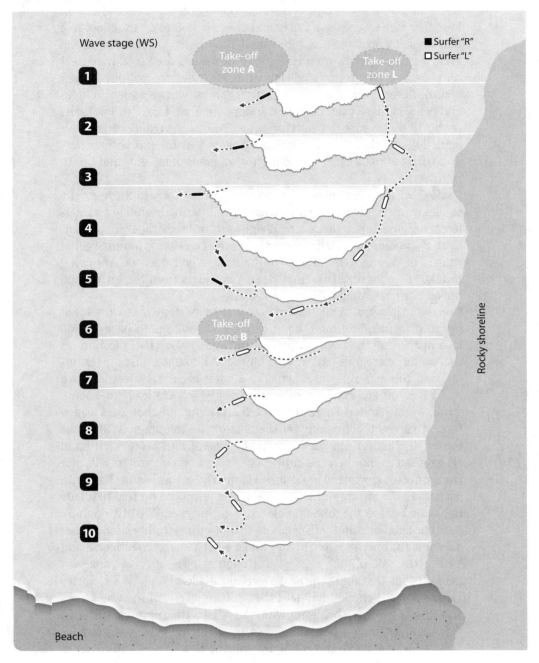

FIGURE 5.2 Creative pathways can yield great surf outings even in a crowd.

Wave stage (WS)

1
2
3
4
5
6
7
8
9
10

Take-off zone **A**

Take-off zone **L**

Take-off zone **B**

■ Surfer "R"
□ Surfer "L"

Rocky shoreline

Beach

Ariel Medel

second group of surfers on the take-off for the right-hand rebreak (B), you are up and riding already, on unbroken wave face, surfing along toward them from well inside, so you have the wave to yourself. There can be forty people total at the location, and you can get ride after ride after ride, all to yourself, because they are so ritualized and so focused on those right-handers that they never pick up on what you are doing. You are observing etiquette perfectly, everyone is happy, and you are getting tons of waves all to yourself. Sure, the initial drop as a left is a bit softer than the right, but you get all of the fun of the rebreak and your total ride is twice as long. That's just one example. Armed with this idea, think outside the box and look for a creative pathway that will help you have a great outing despite the presence of a crowd.

Surfing Safety

Surfing safely starts with you. With some activities, once you take the plunge, anything could happen, and there's not a lot you can do about it. Surfing is not like that. You have great control over the probability of experiencing some sort of mishap and limiting such problems to highly unlikely events—the kind of things that you really shouldn't worry about given you've made the effort to understand the spectrum of hazards and taken every reasonable precaution to avoid them. If you are young and feeling immortal, you may well weigh the risks and decide the rewards of a more dangerous outing are worth it, and purposely go ahead. At least you will know what you are getting into, no surprises. Our goal in this chapter is to cover this hazard spectrum in considerable detail and empower you with ways to minimize your chances of having a problem.

Monitoring Yourself and Your Equipment

We've previously covered many aspects of making good decisions about where and how to surf relative to your age, skill level, and physical condition, and being brutally honest with your self-assessment. You should never surf alone if you can possibly avoid it. Having a partner increases your safety margin manyfold. For example, Wingnut was surfing one day in quite small conditions, executed a snappy dismount (a *kick-out*) to disengage at the end of a ride, and smacked himself right in the head with his own board, knocking himself out cold. His buddies pulled him out of the water. He is reasonably certain he would have died had he been alone. The other take-home lesson is that many of the injuries occur on small days, cheating in to surf in very shallow areas, and likely a more cavalier attitude encouraged by the small waves. Scott once began to execute a last turn in such conditions over a very shallow sandbar, arms splayed, leaned too far, and his left index and middle fingers stuck into the sand so firmly that his body and board wrenched around on this pivot and he fell off. Both fingers were seriously dislocated.

Cardiologist Dr. Percy Aitken of Miami, Florida, makes another very important point. Many people don't realize that heart attacks are surprisingly common between the ages of thirty-five and fifty-five, even among apparently very fit and healthy individuals. He comments that athletes accustomed to constantly pushing themselves hard and nonstop need to change that mentality as they get older, and learn to pause and take a breather when they get huffing and puffing, heart racing, from exertion—even if it does mean subbing out of a ball game for a bit or letting a couple of waves go by. If you've had to battle a bit to get out through the wash zone, or paddle across a rip, stop, sit or lie prone on your board, and take a break when you get to a quiet area. Let your breathing recover and your pulse slow down. Then start looking for your next wave.

The other key aspect Wingnut points out is to check over your equipment before you get in the water. Make sure it's all shipshape and ready for sea. The most important item is one many surfers don't think much about, and that is to carefully check over your leash. Is it abraded or nicked? Are the swivels, rail saver, and attachment cord in good condition? Remember, if that leash breaks at the wrong time (which is usually when it happens), your board could become a deadly torpedo and do someone else and/or their equipment some serious damage. Not only that, the board could get dashed on an inhospitable shoreline or lost entirely. Depending on location, you could have a long swim back as well. Also check to make sure repeated waxings haven't built up an inordinately thick, heavy layer on the deck, which can tend to amalgamate and get slick, and occasionally crumble and come off in chunks from foot pressure. Slipperiness and crumbling can cause you to fall suddenly and unexpectedly, resulting in injury. From time to time put your board out in the sun deck up, let the wax get real soft, and then take the back or "scraper" side of your wax comb and remove all the wax, wiping off the last few smears with an old towel. Re-wax the board as described in detail in Chapter 2.

Wingnut emphasizes the importance of taking care of and looking out for not only yourself but also your surfing partners and all of the other surfers around you. He constantly assesses the other surfers and keeps an eye out. He notes how they look paddling, their skill level in the waves, and their general physical condition, and he constantly watches people on their rides. Are they capable at maneuvering, or are they a hazard? If they wipe out or otherwise terminate the ride, he always looks for a head to pop up, alert and cognizant, and for the rider to recover the board and start paddling. On a number of occasions over the years he has had to rush in and drag surfers out of the water when they did not recover, and even more often he has had to paddle out and tow surfers back in who'd been carried offshore by rip currents and other conditions. A very big part of surfing ethics is to watch out for and help any other surfer who gets into trouble—the fundamental law of the sea.

Surfboards Inflict the Majority of Surfing Injuries

We discussed in the previous chapter the issue of taking great care about where you paddle out, avoiding if at all possible major thoroughfares for riders and the take-off zone, and either turning turtle or free-diving to the bottom if you anticipate being run over. Another very important aspect of paddling out is not to follow behind and in line with another surfer paddling out, and if you do end up behind someone momentarily for whatever reason, Wingnut strongly recommends saying something to let him or her know you are there. If a big wave comes and knocks the person free of his or her board, the board becomes a deadly missile aimed at you (hence the important safety measure to always hold on to your board, except in special circumstances and when you know for certain no one is behind you). Even if the person stays connected, if his or her duck dive doesn't go well, or if the person is on a longboard and the wave is so large that he or she must use the clamshell or clamp move we described, you could still be hit by the person and the board. We also stressed the importance of collision avoidance. The reason for all of these is that the surfboards themselves—those of others, but even more often your own—inflict more surfing injuries than any other hazard.

Shortboards often have sharp noses that can point-load the mass of a fast-moving board, either ridden or unridden, against flesh, muscle, and bone. All boards have fins, and you wouldn't believe the deep, knifelike slashes they can inflict on a human body. Last, getting whacked by the board itself can be like getting hit with a piece of lumber—even if you don't experience any sharp parts. If you take a shot like this in the head in heavy surf, and get knocked cold, it would be easy to drown even if you had a buddy somewhere out in the lineup.

Remember that as you take on bigger, more powerful waves, you will continue to have the odd wipeout. Each time this happens, you are tumbling off a steep, sizable wall, free-falling while attached to what you have just been told is a potentially lethal weapon, your surfboard, by a springy leash. Recall that we emphasized previously the importance of falling flat and away from your board, and covering your head with your arms.

Otherwise, you could "fall on your own sword," so to speak, or come into other hard and damaging contact.

One of the most incredible surf injury stories we've heard involved a very low-probability incident of this very circumstance, told to Scott by Dr. David Green, the renowned Australian emergency physician who dealt with the case. An accomplished surfer was surfing remote Cape Moreton in eastern Australia, wiped out on a large wave, and fell forcefully on his upturned board in the crash. A fin sliced deep into his upper inner thigh, completely severing his femoral artery. His buddies got him to the beach, bleeding copiously, and got in an emergency call via mobile phone. The only thing that saved the surfer's life was that a medevac flight was already airborne and en route to another emergency, and was able to divert for the pickup. The surfer arrived at Gold Coast Hospital near death. Dr. Green revived him with massive infusions and he survived. Very unlikely, but it's always good to realize the possibilities inherent to any undertaking.

Water Hazards and Mishaps with the Seafloor

Watch experienced surfers and you'll occasionally see them begin to take off on a wave and abruptly abort the take-off. Usually this is because they sense that it's too late, too steep, and therefore too risky to try. The consequence can be *going over the falls*, which means getting sucked up into the lip and being projected bodily over the barrel and forcefully down into the impact zone, which, inevitably for big plunging waves, is quite shallow. It's also, as Wingnut reminds us, dangerous to get bottom-slammed, however you wipe out, even in small conditions. One category of surfing injury that is more common than you'd hope is neck, spine, and coccyx (tailbone) fractures from young surfers riding small shallow beach breaks on shortboards, wiping out, and hitting the sand hard.

Of course, rock and coral is worse. Scott once witnessed a very good surfer racing along a wall at a local break that sucks up off a rock shelf, only to experience a close-out (en masse collapse of the entire wave section he was riding) and get literally bounced off the rock platform beyond. The guy picked himself up, duck-dived the next wave, and went back for more. Not two waves later the same exact thing happened again. Miraculously, he fought back out to the take-off zone, but this time he paddled around to the safer break. Asked if he was OK, he said, "Man, that second one *really* hurt. . . . Guess I'll get a few in here."

That same incident on a sharp coral reef could well have resulted in some hunks of meat left behind, and the surfer would definitely not have been going back for more. Coral cuts leave slime and bacteria and, since you are by necessity in the tropics or subtropics when you get them, the climate is ripe for infection. It's very important to clean these wounds, apply antibiotic, and bandage them so they don't get out of control.

Coral reefs can also have lots of 3-D structure and projections, and if you are surfing a reef break on larger-class waves, you might get thrown down on a wipeout, even in fairly deep water, sufficiently to tangle your leash on the reef. This is an excellent moment not to panic. Calmly reach down and undo the Velcro strap at your ankle, then ease back up to the surface. Your board will likely pop up close by; otherwise, you can catch your breath, free-dive back down, and untangle the leash to retrieve it. Large waves can hold you down for quite a while even if you don't get tangled in the bottom, so it's very important to try to get a good deep breath before you submerge, and use as little motion as possible during the hold-down—just relax like a jellyfish. If you flail around, you'll only use more oxygen. When you feel the pressure ease, swim back for the surface. If you've been tumbled and you are disoriented, blow a few bubbles and follow them. They always go up. And be ready to take a big sip of air and resubmerge, because by this time the next big breaker of the set could well be upon you.

We've already touched on assorted hazards involving current—either longshore currents (sweep), rip currents, or hard-running river or tidal currents coursing through a surfing area. Read the current before you enter, and don't waste energy fighting it and trying to swim against a current that begins taking you somewhere you didn't anticipate or want. Wait and watch, paddle calmly *across* the current direction, and call out or wave to get attention before you get too far away in case you need assistance getting back.

Surf Destination Hazards from Bar to Beach

Some of the most serious hazards at any surf area are the bad girls and boys at the beach bar. They may not have ominous big dorsal fins like their more famous maritime counterparts, but they can be just as dangerous, and the odds of an encounter are far higher. And then there's the interaction between those perils and smooth, tropical rum drinks that go down so easily in the afterglow of a great surf session. However, we'll leave you with Oprah on that front and move along. Let's take a quick look at a few other land hazards worthy of mention.

It's essential to check the Centers for Disease Control and Prevention (CDC) in Atlanta, Georgia, or another reliable source for hazards of the area to which you may go surfing. For example, did you know that parasitic meningitis is a risk worldwide in the tropics and subtropics? That's the rat lungworm, *Angiostrongylus cantonensis*, whose infectious larvae are deposited in slime trails left by slugs crawling across lettuce, cabbage, and other vegetables. That means salad is not a good idea within 25 degrees or so of the equator, unless you've soaked the makings yourself for twenty minutes in 10 percent bleach solution (then rinse). See what we mean . . . you didn't know that, did you? (And we only know it by accident.)

Most of us have heard about hepatitis A, B, and C, malaria, giardia, and other malaises. New hepatitis vaccines are available and approved in the United States and other developed countries, and it is foolish indeed not to get them. Malaria prophylactics vary by location, and the CDC can fill you in on what you should take to protect yourself if you're going to an area where this disease is a possibility. The first precaution is to take every available measure not to be bitten by mosquitos—malaria is only one of the afflictions they can carry.

The other main terrestrial category of surf trip infliction that could get serious is skin infections, usually *Staphylococcus* bacteria establishing a new city in cuts, scratches, abrasions, or even the smallest of skin punctures. It pays to scrub down well at the end of each day with a soapy wash cloth, paying particular attention to any wounds, however minor. Then place an adhesive bandage, with antibiotic ointment smeared on the inside, over the wound while you sleep. Meticulous attention to such wounds can save your entire trip. When one of these infections takes off, particularly if it descends to bone, it can become a life-threatening situation overnight, requiring surgery.

Hazards of the Maritime Shallows

So, you've survived your first night at the bar (most of those afflictions won't be apparent right away at any rate), and you have made your way, slightly bleary-eyed, to the water's edge. Without trying to be negative or discouraging, we point out here a few things to keep in mind and how to handle a mishap. A small amount of knowledge and forethought will enable you to avoid nearly all of the potential hazards listed below.

~ **Cone shells and blue-ringed octopuses.** People have problems with these Indo-Pacific mollusks because they're pretty, they live on the beach or in the shallows, and folks tend to pick them up. Neither animal likes it. Cone shells retaliate by extending a dart and impaling the flesh of the holder; blue-ringed octopuses bite with parrot-like beaks. Both transfer potentially lethal venom to the victim. Either event is relatively painless, but within ten minutes the trouble starts— numbness, stiff or tingling lips, followed by paralysis and cessation of breathing. No antivenom is available. Treatment is pressure bandaging and complete immobilization as quickly as possible, followed by prolonged mouth-to-mouth or other artificial resuscitation to prevent death from lack of oxygen. Avoid at all costs.

~ **Stonefish.** Another Indo-Pacific delight, these well-camouflaged bottom dwellers have venomous dorsal spines connected to venom glands, and surfers wading out at Pacific and Indian Ocean islands are particularly vulnerable to stepping on these fishes, getting spiked in the foot by the spines, and receiving a dose of venom. The pain is excruciating. Effective antivenom is available in Australia, but not at most island venues. Best immediate treatment is to bathe and submerse the wound in warm to hot water, which is believed to denature the venom and also disperses it by increasing circulation to the wound area (both good things). Do not use pressure bandaging or immobilization. Shuffling in sandy areas, and avoiding stepping too close to overhangs and rocks where stonefish like to semibury and lie, will help reduce the odds of an encounter.

~ **Stingrays.** These rays occur worldwide, and, like stonefish, get stepped on as they lie motionless, often partially buried, in nearshore shallows. They react by arching their back and raising their tail, which erects a very sharp, serrated barb or set of barbs (depending on the species), stabbing the victim usually in the leg. Venom runs into the wound from a gland or sac via grooves in the stinger, especially from the stump if it breaks off in the flesh. Bathe/submerge in warm to hot water, and get the serrated stinger removed at a medical facility. Shuffle your feet as you walk out and you should never have a problem with stingrays.

~ **Sea urchins.** Also occurring worldwide, sea urchins look like assorted sizes of pin cushion and are prevalent in coral and rocky areas. The spines that project from the ball-like body can be very sharp, hollow, and brittle, easily penetrating flesh through neoprene surf booties. Some are venomous, and all spines should be removed as soon as you can, then clean the wound thoroughly and apply antibiotic.

~ **Coral cuts and stings.** Bodily contact with the tropical and subtropical reefs that generate many of the best waves on the planet can result in cuts or stings that require a bit of special attention, namely removing any foreign matter, cleansing with antibacterial soap, and applying topical antiseptic or antibiotic. In the case of stings, topical and oral cortisones and antihistamines may reduce itching and pain. Best protection is footwear (split-toe surf booties) and any kind of covering—wetsuit, rash guards, long-legged board shorts; the more coverage, the better.

~ **Assorted jellyfish and other hydrozoans.** Jellyfish, and jellyfish-like creatures such as the Portuguese man-o'-war, can cause very painful stings and, in the case of the infamous box jelly mostly found in northern Australia, death. These box jellies are primarily estuarine, most common in summer, and can be avoided by staying away from nearshore areas. They're uncommon on the outer reef areas. Special stinger suits are sold in places like Target and K-Mart in Cairns, Australia, for preventing stings, but the best measure is not to enter the water, ever, in risky areas. Lesser stings from other jellies and hydrozoans can be treated with vinegar and other household remedies (meat tenderizer, lemon juice, sodium bicarbonate), and for Australian blue bottles the top recommendation is application of ice water or ice cubes in lieu of vinegar. The most important step is to pour the vinegar over the tentacles to deactivate them, and then remove them from the skin. Best protection for most jellies is to look around before entering the water—onshore wind in springtime will often blow numbers of blue bottles or man-o'-war and similar organisms to shore, and they'll be visible washed up on the beach. If you see lots, rethink your surfing plans. If there are some, keep an eye out once you are in the water.

~ **Saltwater crocodiles.** These relics of the dinosaur age, and their relatives, occur mostly in estuarine and inshore tropical, as well as some subtropical, environments. The Australian continent seems to have the largest number of annual encounters between people and crocs, usually when the people are pushing safety limits and avoidance guidelines. Occasionally large individuals venture well offshore. Crocodiles also occur in some Indo-Pacific island groups (for example, the Solomon Islands and Papua New Guinea). We are unaware of a crocodile attack on a surfer while in the surf.

Out in the Surf and Ocean

You've been waiting for it . . . the *s* word . . . so here it is: what about *SHARKS*? Statistically, your odds of having a shark problem while surfing are exceedingly low. That said, it really depends on where you are surfing and when you are surfing. Here again, you have a high degree of control over this issue, and having solid knowledge about the topic will help you make the right decisions.

On a worldwide basis, the biggest problem species for surfers are great white sharks, which tend to inhabit cooler, more temperate climes, and, in warmer waters, tiger sharks. These are apex predators (that means they're fast, big, and bad, and they eat human-sized prey without problem). If you think about the top of the food pyramid, this means there's not all that many of them compared to other species and you have to be quite unlucky, in most locations, to have a hungry one come across you sitting there on your board and want to eat you. Bull sharks, bronze whalers, lemon sharks, great hammerheads, and assorted other species of coastal migratory and reef sharks, most notably the highly territorial Indo-Pacific gray reef shark (*Carcharhinus amblyrhynchos*), can also pose problems for surfers. But before we get started on shark stories, each of which contains a take-home lesson, let's list assorted conditions that can sharply reduce this risk for you:

~ **Find regular surf spots.** If you are contemplating a surf spot frequented regularly by surfers, and no one has ever been bitten or attacked, this usually means your chances of a shark experience at this location are infinitesimal. For example, Scott's current location in eastern Australia features abundant large dangerous sharks nearby, but most of the main surfing beaches have shark nets and baited shark lines. There have been no problems at these beaches. It's not that the sharks can't get to the beach; it's just that the nets and hooks likely pick off enough of the ones who wander in to keep a lid on it. Many people surf these areas almost constantly and no one remembers a single attack since the shark gear was deployed long ago.

~ **Avoid shark-problem surf spots.** Know the history of the place you're thinking about surfing. Surfers avoid some places entirely due to past problems. Other well-known spots have had fatal attacks, but so rarely that large numbers of surfers view their individual chances of becoming a victim as small compared to the rewards. Find out about it and decide for yourself.

~ **Avoid early morning and evening outings.** The crack of dawn and when the sun is getting low near the end of the day are prime feeding times for sharks, fish, and other sea creatures. It's riskier to surf at these times than when the sun is higher. Many of us have been having a ball in excellent surf, and, swept away by the moment, surfed through sunset and into the night for just a bit. It's exhilarating but not something you want to do more than a couple of times, or ever if you're smart.

~ **Avoid schools of bait fish.** If you go to your favorite surf spot and see large, dark balls of baitfish, perhaps marked by diving seabirds, or you are already out and suddenly you are surrounded by schools of fish, relocate. Schools of fish attract predators.

~ **Know that murky water is more risky.** One could hardly blame a shark, barracuda, or even large bluefish (called tailor in Australia) for taking a snap at the flash of a pale hand stroking through very murky water, adapted as they are to reacting quickly to stimuli in order to feed and make a living.

~ **Investigate new or isolated locations before surfing there.** Go snorkel around the surf spot for a while and see who's around. Are there lots of fish at this location, indicating a vibrant marine community with plenty of food to attract and hold sharks? Any territorial reef sharks patrolling? Are they at all aggressive to you? How close is the drop-off to deep ocean water? Big sharks often patrol oceanic walls and make forays into the adjacent shallows to feed.

~ **Wingnut says there's never been a recorded attack on a longboarder.** Longboarders say shortboarders are the go, who in turn say boogie boarders are the real shark food, although unfortunately there are a number of recorded attacks on shortboarders, too. Wingnut claims no attacks yet on longboarders, which does make sense, considering the much larger profile presented. Just one more reason to go longboarding.

~ **Surf with company.** Surfing with other surfers around sharply reduces your odds of becoming prey to a shark, starting with a 50 percent reduction, all else equal, with the presence of your first fellow surfer.

~ **If you see a threatening shark (size and/or behavior), get out of the water.** If you see a large shark, or you are approached closely by even a smaller shark, the prudent thing to do is to leave, unless you positively identify the shark as a nondangerous species (for example, members of the nurse shark family, Indo-Pacific white-tip reef sharks, and other sluggish species).

~ **Don't surf at all, or be very cautious about surfing at or near, a seal or sea lion colony.** In cooler waters, marine mammal concentrations may be feeding stations for great whites.

~ **Don't surf at a concentrated area for sea turtle nesting during nesting season.** Sea turtles crawl ashore to dig nests and deposit their eggs on sandy beaches in the subtropics and tropics. Large tiger sharks like to eat these adult turtles. They snatch them and chomp repeatedly until they break the shell. If you can surf away from the concentrations, just down the beach in some areas, you're better off.

~ **Be aware of seasonal concentrations of migrating coastal sharks.** Large bull sharks, for example, move in to certain beach areas along the Gulf Coast of Florida in summer to breed and bear young. They've been responsible for a number of fatal attacks in recent years on people in the surf.

~ **Avoid paddling across inlets, river mouths, and passes, particularly in the wake of a fishing trawler.** These high-current conduits are commonly feeding stations for, and areas of greater abundance of, sharks. At commercial fishing ports, these sharks become attuned to the presence of shrimp trawlers and the free meals often available as they sort the catch. Consequently, they'll follow the trawlers like dogs. Paddling across the wake of a trawler, especially an incoming one, increases your chance of being in the vicinity of large sharks.

Shark Stories

The idea of being attacked by a shark is highly emotional. Most people, including surfers, have little or no practical experience with sharks, and whatever information they do have often suffers from questionable reliability. Professional fishermen, divers, long-distance sailors, island or coastal natives, and other persons with considerable sea time and exposure make up those with the most shark experience.

Here again, let's not sugarcoat the subject. If a large hungry shark gets a bead on you and wants you, chances are you'll never know what hit you. They can move in very fast bursts and their dental equipment is mind-boggling. Therefore, if you see a big shark first, this is a good sign, because it means it's likely not all that interested—if it were, it would already have grabbed you. Chances are you can ease away. This is not necessarily the case with smaller territorial species, most notably Indo-Pacific gray reef sharks. They attack humans not out of hunger but because they are territorial. They'll circle and approach, and the final warning is humping the back, pectoral fins down, mouth yawning, head swaying—at this point you have very little time left to leave the area. The species grows to just over eight feet (about 255 cm maximum), yet even small individuals can be quite aggressive. Losing a crescent of leg flesh or having a major artery severed in a territorial attack, particularly at a remote location, can be life-threatening.

How likely is an event like this? Again, it depends entirely on where you are. There are certain island surf breaks that you simply can't surf because of the nasty gray reef sharks that call particular reef corners and passes home. Such spots are generally very well known by the locals and no one surfs them, because the chances of an attack are extremely high. In short, you shouldn't have a problem like this when visiting an inhabited area for the purpose of surfing. And even in the absence of local advice, if you were to snorkel such an area first you would soon become aware of the sharks as they are very alert to intruders and will show themselves and their intentions very quickly.

What snorkeling around wouldn't tell you much about is the probability of a wandering tiger shark, great white, or other species cruising in from deeper water and developing an interest in having you for a snack. Historical incidents for the area would be highly significant, as would proximity to marine mammal colonies or other abundant food, deep drop-offs, seasonal migration pathways, and the presence of whales. Big sharks accompany whales, looking for opportunities to attack young calves and other vulnerable individuals. Some whales will pass very, very close to shore—for example, humpback whales migrating in winter months from Antarctica to tropical Pacific islands and up along the coast of Australia to the Great Barrier Reef. If you spot a whale spout out a ways from your surf location, odds are there's a large shark somewhere in the vicinity as well. Whether or not this shark would tend to wander in and bother people surfing is anyone's guess. One way to take the guesswork out of it is to get out of the water.

Tropical islands frequently feature steep oceanic drop-offs near shore, and if such a drop-off lies along a pathway patrolled regularly by big sharks, and if people routinely enter the water near this drop-off, there will likely be a history of problems at this location. There is one particular Pacific island resort area, for example, meeting these conditions. Guests snorkel the shallows adjacent to the resort, which abruptly plummet into deep water out a ways from shore. Of course, this drop-off is quite spectacular and teeming with marine life. Unfortunately, although many such areas wouldn't be a problem, large tiger sharks are rather abundant along this particular wall. Consequently, snorkelers have been repeatedly attacked in this area by tiger sharks. Once more, reducing the risk of shark attack depends on asking the right questions, assessing the situation, and making sound decisions.

The last point is that swimmers and surfers choose to immerse themselves in a dynamic environment home to many sea creatures. There are plenty of sharks around in many such areas, going about their business, which most of the time has nothing whatsoever to do with people. Most shark species are adapted to feed on fish and invertebrates considerably smaller and with an entirely different profile to people on surfboards. Even areas where the most dangerous sharks are abundant have incredibly low attack rates relative to the number of sharks present. A good example of this was a recent interview with an Australian surfer and fisherman who kept losing fish to sharks while surf fishing in the vicinity of Stockton, New South Wales, Australia, along a very popular stretch of surfing beach. He and his buddies decided to bring out some heavier tackle and steel leaders to see what they could find out about the culprits. They rigged up a big-game chair on the front bull bar of a four-wheel drive vehicle and actually began paddling big baits out beyond the breakers on their surfboards. They began repeatedly hooking big sharks that they couldn't stop. Finally they landed one—a great white. As they got better at it, they continually landed great whites, and it got so they reportedly never waited longer than twenty minutes for the strike, often while the guy who'd paddled the bait out was still paddling back in. Remember, this is at a favorite surf beach. Well, great whites are protected now, so when the media found out and publicized their hobby, government conservation officials quickly shut them down. Nonetheless, these fellows still cruised up and down the beach and, now alerted to the high abundance of sharks, scanned the surf carefully. They found they could actually spot individual great whites cruising around—up to twenty-five over a relatively short section of beach sometimes.

When asked how this had affected his surfing habits, the ringleader commented in effect, "Well, I'm much more sensitive about not surfing early or late, preferring to surf when there's others about to reduce my own odds," and, in typical surfing spirit, "unless of course the surf conditions are really perfect." This reminded Scott of visiting the remote pearl camp at Penrhyn Island, in the central equatorial Pacific region of the Cook Islands, managed by surfer Mike Grubnau. The reef passes Mike surfed regularly by himself were packed with gray reef sharks and full of other sea life. Scott was incredulous and asked him how he dealt with the sharks. Mike replied, "Oh, when they get pushy and start bumping into me, I give them a good kick." Such places are famous for tiger sharks, among other reasons because they like to come in and eat the gray reef sharks, and when asked about that Mike said, "I've only had one incident with a tiger bothering me. I kicked him hard and he swam off. I got a few more waves and called it a day." Maybe Wingnut is onto something here, because Mike surfs a longboard. A friend of Scott's buddy Eric Vogt wasn't quite so lucky. He was boogie boarding alone at Kauai, Hawaii, paddling back out after a ride, when suddenly a big tiger loomed out of an oncoming wave, jaws agape, straight for him. He had time only to shove his boogie board forward as the tiger snapped at him, cutting the board in half, and completely severing both of his hands (neither of which was seen again). The big shark circled but didn't press the attack further. Eric's friend managed to make it back to the beach, and miraculously scaled a steep path back up the cliff, made it to the nearest house, and collapsed as he knocked on the door, where the alerted residents called an ambulance. (Incidentally, this individual ended up designing prostheses for a living.)

Similarly, the big-shark attacks on surfers are sudden, explosive events that once triggered would be difficult to defend or avoid. Witnesses report views of a fast, whitewater event and that's usually the last anyone sees of the victim. Recently, however, a diver in South Australia, grabbed by a great white, poked it in the eye and got spat back out. In another incident not long before, a diver's buddies watched as a great white calmly approached and took the diver, who was still visibly struggling and poking at the shark as it swam off, never letting go. Attacks on surfers usually haven't appeared to afford this opportunity, although recently a great white released a young Californian surfer after the initial bite. One South Australian surf spot suffered fatal great white attacks on surfers on consecutive days a short time ago.

Stories like these illustrate the possibilities, although they are akin to sensationalist news channels in big cities dramatizing car accidents and particularly gruesome crimes. Statistically, with millions of people packed into a given area, something nasty will happen every day. To dwell on this and inflate the realistic probability of personally experiencing such an event is to behave irrationally. Follow the guidelines in this chapter and you'd probably be more likely to be struck by lightning the next time you step outside than you'd be to have a shark problem while surfing. Irrational fears can really get in the way of having fun and enjoying life to the hilt.

Bringing along a well-stocked medical kit, adjusted to your location and remoteness from medical care, can boost your safety margins across the board of possible mishaps. Appendix B addresses this topic in more detail.

Moving Up

INTERMEDIATE AND ADVANCED TOOLS AND TECHNIQUES

7

Think of this chapter as putting the finishing touches on a painting. Chapter 4 completed the framework of broad strokes, Chapters 5 and 6 ensured your happiness and safety while becoming adept at executing these basics, and now you are ready for us to fill in the final details so that you have a masterpiece. Presenting them earlier would have risked obscuring the framework. Now we can safely switch over to the fine brushes and more subtle lines and hues, which will lead very naturally into a detailed distillation, in our next chapter, of the full spectrum of equipment that makes it possible for you to bring it all to life.

Early on we made the important point that nearly every surfer learns on a longboard, and so should you. Then what? Many surfers get hooked on the superior versatility, wave-catching ability, and ride length; the greater number of days you get to go surfing; the greater number, size range, and variety of waves you get to ride; and the cruising, relaxed, effortless style of surfing, with more time for smooth, varied maneuvers. As you go down in board size and more to the pointy-nosed, exaggerated-rocker, thinner and narrower shortboards, your equipment demands more frenetic, constant, and powerful driving and maneuvering to stay up to speed. It demands more powerful waves and cleaner, steeper wave faces. It locks you into place in a flat-footed stance. And it locks your maneuvers into a more narrow and repetitive repertoire of bottom turn, top turn, cutback, over and over again. On the flip side, shortboards really come into their own on bigger waves, they allow you to take off and ride in much bigger, steeper conditions, and they are ideal for tube riding in hollow conditions. They're made for it. Longboards aren't. It's still fair to say that longboards successfully surf a much broader range of wave types, and you can take on big hollow waves with them too, but you're better off downsizing and using the right equipment for the waves you choose to ride.

Wingnut was asking longboard phenomenon Joel Tudor about this one day on the north shore of Oahu, Hawaii, and Joel put it something like this: "I like to surf my full-sized longboard in waves up to about shoulder-high, and then I think it's ideal to begin going down in board size. Some of the intermediate sizes and styles of boards in the 7′–8′ range are a great way of making the transition down to the smaller shortboards. They still have greater volume and width, they're smoother and less chaotic to keep moving and to generate speed, and they'll still cruise. If you go straight down from a 9'6" longboard to a 6'6" shortboard, it can make you feel like you're on a tippy little toothpick and it might take awhile to make that transition. While some of the stuff you can do on the modern-day shortboard is spectacular and takes great skill, they demand frenetic, fast-paced work. On a day-in, day-out basis, it's not my cup of tea. I'd rather take a little more time."

To this we'd add an important note. There's a way to cheat. Buy a *fish*. This is a wider, higher-volume shortboard with flat rocker that is almost like lopping off the front two-thirds of a full-sized longboard, and guess what? They paddle much more easily than a high-performance shortboard, they catch waves almost as readily as a longboard, yet they're much smaller and more maneuverable like a shortboard. To top it off, they have a distinctly deliberate maneuvering characteristic, allowing you more time and more forgiveness. This is an excellent option for acquiring shortboard experience in, say, the 6'6" to 6'10" lengths, in weaker, gentler conditions and having a ball.

Much more on this in the next chapter. Now, have you noticed what we've done to you? We actually slipped in all of the basic technique for riding either a longboard or a shortboard in Chapter 4 by specifically pointing out the differences between the two for the fundamental maneuvers. You already know how to ride either a longboard or a shortboard, whether or not you've tried the latter. We'll now build on that foundation and take you to the top of both styles, then in the next chapter we'll shop 'til we drop.

More on Reading Waves

As with any surfing endeavor, advancing and perfecting skills has everything to do with choosing the wave. Beach breaks can be excellent for this. A sandy bottom and shoreline allow you to take more chances because it's less likely to result in damage to you or your board. The incoming peaks tend to be more variable, less predictable, and more challenging to read, anticipate, get position on, and surf well. This tends to spread the surfers out more and afford more opportunity for capitalizing on waves off to one side of a crowd. Beach waves are often fast and may commonly break more top to bottom, so you need to be more alert, quicker, and organized with a plan of attack. Everything is happening more quickly; you need to read the incoming swell faster, pop up rapidly, and execute a fast first turn in order to make the wave. Of these, the key is that speedy, smooth pop-up; already knowing if you are taking it as a left or a right is also essential.

Reef breaks, if we define them in a broad sense to mean any wave created by fixed, hard bottom features, be they coral or rocks, either submerged in various configurations out from a shoreline or in connection with a point, all have one thing in common: predictability. Because the wave-creating object is solid and fixed in place, the waves break over and over again in exactly the same spot. This ease of reading draws tighter-packed crowds of surfers and often more competition for waves. The repetitiveness of the wave break, however, allows anticipation and planning of how you will run the wave. For example, the wave may break along a shelving hard formation that has a shallow section near the end of the run. Each wave stands up and gets quite hollow in this section, then breaks. Therefore, your goal is to punch through the run fast enough to make it through that final jack-up and collapse. If such a circumstance is producing a tube section, then you can adjust your speed and set up position accordingly.

The ultimate circumstance for perfecting skills may well be the wave machine. If you have the money to consistently rent out a facility with a wave machine, you can program in the wave type, size, and frequency, and practice specific skills over and over again in exactly the same conditions. The take-offs are at precisely the same spot each time, and the tube, for example, develops at exactly the same location and in the identical manner. For those of us on normal budgets, however, frequenting a reef break will offer a similar opportunity to practice in a real-world setting.

Additional Skills for Getting Out

One major advantage of true shortboards is that they give you the ability to duck dive. When you are paddling out on a longboard in larger surf, and you look up as a big set of waves approaches, knowing it's going to break in front of you, you might develop a kind of siege mentality. Turning turtle might not be feasible as the power of the waves will likely tear the board out of your hands. That leaves the option of hanging off the side and clamping a section of rail up near the nose to your chest, but let's face it, you're going to get hammered. Not so with a shortboard. You simply paddle hard straight for the wave, execute a smooth, deep duck dive, and lose very little ground as you surface out the back of the swell and keep paddling (Figure 7.1). No big deal.

Getting out efficiently is all about saving energy. In less extreme waves, here are a couple of additional longboard tricks, the *sitting pop-over* and the *stand-up pop-over* (Photos 7.1 and 7.2). Use these when the incom-

FIGURE 7.1 Profile of a duck dive.

a Paddle strongly directly at the oncoming wave.

b Use this forward momentum, a decisive shift of weight forward, and downward angle to plunge down into the wave base.

c The forward energy of the wave on your angled back and board deck pushes you farther down. Begin to level off, and shift your body aft.

d This arcs the nose upward, and you pop harmlessly out the back of the wave.

Ariel Medel

ing whitewater is too big for pushing through by raising your body on straight arms to let it pass under your chest. You would actually be surprised at the size of waves to which you can apply these techniques, and they require less energy than turning turtle (and of course you don't get that dunking, particularly beneficial if the water is cold).

PHOTO 7.1 Wingnut setting up for a sitting pop-over in whitewater a little too big for a push-through. His weight is aft, raising the nose of the board above the leading slope of the incoming whitewater. As the whitewater hits the underside of the nose, the forward part of the board will start to rise sharply. Wingnut counters this by leaning forward. At the peak of the whitewater passage, he'll launch bodily forward and grasp the rails well ahead of the board's midpoint, come down the back side of the wave, and be in paddling position, ready to continue out.

PHOTO 7.2 Wingnut executing a standing pop-over. The important part of this maneuver is to paddle hard and develop some board speed just prior to popping up to a standing position, far enough aft to get that nose angled upward, over whitewater or, as in this case, through the thin upper lip of the collapsing wave (a). Wingnut's momentum carries him up and through the wave (b), as he leans forward to counter the force of the water on the forward section of the board. Coming down the back side, he then grasps the rails and begins dropping back down to a prone paddling position on the board (c). This skill, as you can see from the photos, will punch you neatly and with relatively little effort through oncoming waves without losing ground. The standing pop-over will handle larger oncoming waves than the sitting pop-over, which handles larger incoming waves than the push-through we demonstrated in Chapter 4.

Take-Offs

Taking off on the wave includes paddling on, popping up, and starting your first maneuver. There are three basic methods for maximum success:

- **Fade turn.** This is basically for longboards only, applies generally to soft point break waves, and comes in two variations. First, you can take off at a slight angle opposite to the direction you intend to go, slanting down and attaining maximum speed while prone, then pop to your feet so you can then get maximum bottom-turn drive out of the momentum. The second method is called a *high fade*, and in this case you paddle on at the angle and in the direction you intend to go, feel the board begin to surge, then shift weight aft to hang the board high in the wave with the forward half out of the water, then quickly pop up and turn high in the lip of the wave (and many will then go straight to the nose ride). In either case, the main purpose of a fade is to delay and buy time so that the wave energy develops or sets up in front of you. Please go back to Photos 4.9, 4.10, and 4.11 to see a fade turn using the first method described.
- **Straight bottom turn.** Good for all boards, this technique is applicable in bigger beach break waves, for example, as opposed to soft point break waves. Here you paddle on aiming straight down the wave face (90 degrees to the line of the wave crest), pop up, and execute a hard turn at the bottom of the wave face. Please go back to Photos 4.20 a–b to see a good example of a nice hard bottom turn.
- **Angled take-off.** Applicable to the biggest, fastest waves, for all boards, you paddle on at an angle, pop up, and race straight on that track, or line, across the wave face. This gains you the greatest lateral distance in the least time and would often be the method used to set up a tube ride in bigger surf (Photo 7.3).

Another trick you can incorporate is to get into the best estimated position for take-off on an incoming swell, turn to face shore, tilt the nose skyward, submerge the board with pressure, release it so the board's buoyancy launches it while reestablishing paddle position to send it forward instead of up, and pop up. This is a *no-paddle take-off* and it works well for longboards and shortboards. Regardless of exactly how you do it, this is the hardest part of surfing, getting that positioning and timing perfected for efficient, consistent wave capture.

PHOTO 7.3 Here Wingnut has used an angled take-off. Even though it's not a big, fast wave, this method was useful because it enabled him to take off very late, right off the steep section of the breaking lip, then shoot off on a line high in the wave and therefore maximize his speed. Also look ahead to the tube-riding section.

Bottom Turns, Top Turns, Reentries, and Cutbacks

A bottom turn is the first big turn of the ride, either a forehand (frontside) or backhand (backside) turn involving strong execution of the mechanics we've already learned using the speed and momentum from that first drop down the wave face. Your bottom turn sets up the rest of the wave.

Here it's worth reemphasizing that one of the main differences between turning a shortboard and a longboard is that your upper-body rotation—swinging of the arms, torso, waist, and hips—in combination with back foot pressure to form a pivot point, and front foot pressure to put the brakes on when you've swung around as far as you wish, is what initiates and controls the turn in the case of a shortboard. Body rotation is at the very least simultaneous to, if not preceding, weighting on the feet and leaning of the body. For turning a longboard, it's the other way around—

you start the turn with foot pressure and leaning and rotate your body as a follow-through. One friend accustomed to a shortboard illustrated this point very graphically when he hopped on a longboard, abruptly swung his arms and upper body expecting to initiate a bottom turn, and launched himself off the board, which continued to go straight.

On either a longboard or a shortboard, a pop-up is often quickly followed by a shift in weight aft, that is, exerting pressure on the back foot, and setting up that bottom turn. Bottom turns on a frontside wave are easier, because all of that differential pressure control, with most on the back foot but maintaining the right light pressure on the front foot, is through the balls of the feet and the toes, and you are leaning forward (see Photos 4.20 a–b). On the backside bottom turns, it's all transmitted down through your knees and to your heels, and you are leaning backward, not forward (Photo 7.4). Thus backside will likely feel less natural than frontside at first. With practice you can get good at both. Longboarders have the additional option of using the drop-knee technique for bottom turning.

PHOTO 7.4 Setting up a backside bottom turn on a small wave. Note the pressure Wingnut is applying through his heels and by leaning backward.

Very often riders choose to bottom turn so that they are angling back up the wave face. Longboards tend to take a gentler angle and smoother line back up the wave, whereas shortboarders, by swinging their upper body harder and putting greater pressure on the back (pivot) foot, can wrench around sharply and carve more radical turns. Regardless of how quickly you make it back up to the top of the wave, you now need to turn back down or you'll continue right up and off the lip of the wave like a rocket. Here again, it's the same mechanics, but you turn in the opposite direction of your bottom turn to come angling back down the wave face. Shortboarders and progressive-style longboarders have developed the art of bottom-turning hard up the wave face, smacking the thin upper lip of the wave hard, beginning top-turn execution at just the right moment to fly up, board partially or completely out of the water, and then reconnecting, angling back down the wave. This is an advanced maneuver called a *reentry* (Australians of course apply a diminutive, calling these *reos*). A related maneuver is the floater, where the surfer angles up fast for the lip and launches at a shallower angle than when hitting the lip for a reentry; surfs along the top of the wave crest (often the top curvature of the falls or at least a broken white crumbling section of crest), usually flying along briefly and lightly on the air-water interface; and then drops back down the wave face.

From time to time in a given ride, coming out of a bottom turn and angling along the wave face will carry the surfer quickly well out along the wave face, out of that steep portion closest to the curl, an area called *the pocket*. Surfers correct this overrun by exaggerating the next top turn to continue all the way around so that rather than angling down and away from the pocket, they are angling down and back toward the pocket, followed by a sharp turn back to continue in the direction of the breaking wave, but now back in the steeper part of the wave face closer to the pocket (Photo 7.5). Generally speaking, the shortboarders tend to make much sharper, harder, racier, and more violent turns and cutbacks than the longboarders, although the progressive longboarders surfing high-performance boards armed with tri-fin arrangements force this equipment through shortboard-style repertoires (Photo 7.6). Both pump speed and power from their boards for these maneuvers, flexing legs and knees to execute the most forceful possible flat-foot turns. Longboarders can also use the drop-knee technique for forcing a strong, decisive cutback. The most important thing to remember about the cutback is that the purpose is to set up the next move. Trimming and stalling are also critical to setting up ensuing sections of the ride.

PHOTO 7.5 This photo sequence demonstrates the dynamics of using momentum from a frontside bottom turn to come up a wave face and then execute a forceful backside top turn (a, b), continuing to carry it through into a cutback (c, d, e), and then turning back to continue on the wave perfectly positioned in the pocket (f, g).

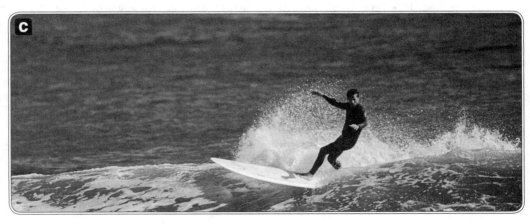

PHOTO 7.6 Progressive longboarders and shortboarders tend to force more violent cutbacks and other maneuvers, driving hard and flat-footed off their fins and the back of their rails.

Trimming

The development and maintenance of speed on a wave is the essence of surfing well. It leads to everything else. It confers the ability to perform reentries and cutbacks, set up tube rides or nose rides, and make it through sections on *speed tracks*. We already know that proper basic trim is critical for a surfboard to shoot along efficiently on a plane, but when we discuss creating and sustaining speed during a ride, one major dichotomy in surfing styles is (1) mostly staying flat-footed and pumping and driving for power off the back rails and fins of your board or (2) carefully fine-tuning and adjusting trim for an optimal glide path, high up in the wave, traveling effortlessly at the maximum speed for the board (in boating terms, hull speed). This art of trimming is relevant to both shortboards and longboards, and once you have established it you can just stand there, relaxed, upper body still, hands down at your sides, perfectly adjusted and feeling the speed. The *trim spot*, or position, on a longboard is forward of middle, near where your chest would be as you paddle out. One traditional-style option once you have reached perfect trim is to establish a parallel foot stance, knees bent, arms in front of you, the way Robert August made famous at Cape St. Francis, South Africa, in the original *Endless Summer* (Photos 7.7 and 7.8).

We know shortboarders mostly trim using differential weighting applied to flat feet, or at the most, with very small shuffles. Longboarders shuffle too. For longer-distance weight transfers, shuffling can be jerky or less smooth, which may be one reason longboarders long ago developed the art of walking up and down the centerline to adjust trim. Walking is one of the techniques that separates longboarding from shortboarding and is an integral part of setting up other longboarding techniques such as nose riding, in addition to merely maintaining trim (Photo 7.9).

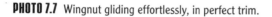

PHOTO 7.7 Wingnut gliding effortlessly, in perfect trim.

PHOTO 7.8 In trim, parallel stance.

PHOTO 7.9 Wingnut starts from way back on the board, stalling to set up the move forward (a). He then begins taking small, smooth crossover steps precisely along the centerline of the board, maintaining the correct lateral angle of his feet while doing so (b, c). As he approaches the trim spot of the board (d, e, f), the board is accelerating. Perched at the trim spot (g) he attains maximum speed, which can then permit a little trip out to the nose to hang five (h, i).

(continued)

Walking also demonstrates in a large-scale, easy-to-notice manner the effect of changing trim and how you can use such changes to decelerate, or stall, as well as accelerate, in instances where a pause can allow time for the wave to set up in front of you.

Stalling

Whereas the term *trimming* normally applies to speeding up, stalling is slowing down. Depending on what is happening with a wave, especially on slower-developing point breaks, it can be very useful to stall, whether you are shortboarding or longboarding. The first three methods described here apply equally to both; the last, the nose stall, is for longboarders (Photo 7.10).

~ **Check stall.** Put pressure on the back foot to dig in the tail, lift the board, and squat to plow water and slow down, then reestablish trim by pressing again on your front foot to continue at speed. On a shortboard, this sequence will be brief; on a longboard, you can draw it out for longer if needed, often followed by walking forward to run down the wave.

~ **Mini-cutback.** Put even more pressure on the back foot to lift the front of the board out, then pivot it only 10 to 15 degrees off course, back and forth if necessary, as opposed to a full cutback.

~ **Full cutback.** As detailed previously, you are doing a full U-turn to get back to the desired part of a wave and then turning back again.

~ **Nose stall.** Going to the nose slows the board down, and in the next section we'll see how variations in what you do while you're up there will allow you to slow the board down more or less, depending on what you are seeing and anticipating down the line on the wave.

PHOTO 7.10 Coming off a long, gradual fade turn, which is in itself a delaying maneuver (a–c), notice how Wingnut is looking down the line, watching what is developing. He buys more time with a check stall (d, e), rides up the steepening wave face and uses the lip to execute a full cutback (f–j), still looking along the building wave in front of him, then begins a frontside turn to continue (k).

(continued)

Nose Riding

Nose riding is the consummate longboard surfing skill. It means that you have positioned your board so beautifully and so well that it will keep surfing along with you perched out on the nose. Nose riding is to the longboarder what tube riding, covered in the next section, is to the shortboarder. These two arts are the quintessential, signature expressions of riding longboards and shortboards.

Nose riding is broadly defined as surfing from the front third of your board, ahead of the trim spot, and of course the experts sometimes define it a bit more strictly to say a true nose ride must have some toes curled over the front of the nose. How many toes and where your weight is determines whether it's a hang five (the toes of one foot over the nose), cheater five (five toes over, but squatting way back on the back foot with front foot extended), or hang ten (toes of both feet all curled over the nose). When moving back and forth from the trim spot to a hang five, switching to a cheater five to speed back up and ride awhile, back to the trim spot, then maybe forward for a hang ten, walking is the key to this dynamic equilibrium. Anytime your weight is centered forward the board is slowed in direct proportion to the distance between you and the trim spot. Thus the hang ten is the strongest nose stall technique, the hang five is second, and the cheater five is so mild that you may achieve stability for the longest stretches since your weight is so far back toward the trim spot (Photos 7.11–7.13).

Good nose riders use three main techniques to set it up:

- **First turn method.** Coming out of a fade turn or straight bottom turn, arc around to travel back up the wave face at a slight angle to achieve position, then walk forward to the nose. The board will continue up the face with you out on the nose, settle high, tail submerged in the crest, and angle off and along the wave face maintaining this high, semistalled position (Photo 7.14).
- **Tail stall method.** You're up and riding. Get your weight back on the tail to stall, allowing the wave to steepen and build in front of you. Then pulse your weight well back to really stall by digging the tail in hard, and immediately walk to the nose. The board will accelerate as you pass over the trim spot, which will help it to tolerate the deceleration of going to the nose. Once more, the tail stays dug in, the board settles into equilibrium high in the wave, and it will cruise nicely for some time with you out on the nose (Photo 7.15).
- **Angled take-off method.** On larger, more powerful waves, you can take off at an angle, pop up, and immediately run forward to the nose,

PHOTO 7.11 Hanging five.

PHOTO 7.12 The cheater five.

PHOTO 7.13 Hanging ten.

PHOTO 7.14 The first turn method of setting up and performing a nose ride. Wingnut comes out of a tail-heavy frontside turn (a), angles up the wave face, and starts the walk forward (b). The board accelerates as he approaches (c) and passes over (d, e) the trim spot, buying him enough speed to continue out to the nose (f, g) and hang five. This slows the board down, but because of his precise setup and subsequent optimal positioning high in the wave with the tail sucked into the lip, he attains a near-equilibrium nose ride glide path. Note that this relatively small, slow wave permits small steps up the board's centerline.

(continued)

picking up even more speed, and execute your drop-in while out on the nose (Photos 7.16 and 7.17).

The angled take-off method illustrates and introduces a very interesting point about nose riding. You can actually do quite a bit of surfing while out on the nose of your board. Not only can you drop in, but you can also make adjustments by subtle weight shifts and body movements

PHOTO 7.15 The tail stall method of setting up and performing a nose ride. Note this wave is a bit larger and more powerful, yielding sufficient board speed to establish a nose ride from a straight tail stall. In frame (a), Wingnut has started the move forward from the sunken tail, gaining considerable speed and really firing along the wave face as he approaches (b) and passes over the trim spot (c, d), continuing to the nose for the hang five (e, f). Note that this faster, more powerful wave demands larger steps up the board's centerline.

PHOTO 7.16 The angled take-off method of setting up and performing a nose ride. This sequence involves a considerably larger and more powerful wave than the two preceding sequences. Here Joel Tudor takes off directly on an angle (a), takes a couple of fast, large steps (b, c), and is very quickly to the nose and hanging five (d).

PHOTO 7.17 Wingnut demonstrates the technique for the angled take-off method of nose riding, making it to the nose in two big, fast steps. No matter the maneuver, the bigger and faster the wave, the more quickly you need to execute it.

incorporating arm positions and leanings (see Photo 7.16d). On a beach break, for example, you may need to adjust the line of your board to compensate for waves that aren't perfectly consistent, orderly peelers. So you're out there on the nose, and you are applying more or less pressure and weight on your back and front feet, and leaning by varying the weight distribution from the toes and balls of your feet to your heels, slowing down, speeding up, and turning. Note that back foot weighting is all-important in nose riding (Remember the joke about "it's all in the wrist"? Well, speed control in nose riding is "all in the back foot"). We'll get more into board technology in the next chapter, but we'll just mention here that a single fin is "looser" and more forgiving for this kind of work than a tri-fin arrangement.

Tube Riding

Tube riding for many surfers is the ultimate experience, and it explains at least partially the enthusiasm for the shortboard. They're perfect for maintaining trim position very effectively in hollow conditions. Why can't a longboard do it? Well, remember that the trim spot on a longboard, due to the greater length of the rails, is well forward of the middle of the board. The "tube ride trim spot" may be even a bit further forward than a "normal" trim spot, so in those hollow conditions the tail of the board really wants to let go. You generally can't stay in the right spot long enough to tube ride as effectively on a longboard as you can on a shortboard without popping that tail out, which is an instant wipeout in those conditions.

But wait a minute, you say, what about that footage of Joel Tudor getting some longer tube rides at Pipeline, and Wingnut surfing Cloud Break in Fiji? These are special circumstances, exceptions rather than the rule, and remember Wingnut ate it big time for the footage they did get of him making it work out occasionally on full-sized longboards. He took it on bravely, fitting a station wagon into a slot better suited for a Porsche. Regular folks, like Scott, must recognize this for what it was, a heroic effort by a world-class expert, not something a normal surfer should necessarily "try at home." And just because longboards aren't magnificently suited to tube riding the way they are to nose riding, it is a tribute to their versatility that you can still tube ride and have a lot of fun with it on your longboard, particularly in smaller conditions.

Whether you are beginning to tube ride on a longboard or a shortboard, try these three steps to get started:

- **Head dip.** You are surfing along on a small, frontside wave, right at the position where the lip is beginning to curl over and break. Rather than drifting out and letting it wash down your body, bend over, knees fairly straight, and dip your head into the curl, maybe getting it just under the protruding little lip projecting out (Photo 7.18).
- **Little cover-up.** Same scenario as the head dip, with just a little bit bigger wave: you position back or stall to allow the pocket to catch up to you, and you hold a line in tight (*pulled in*) to the wave base. Since it's still a small wave, you then squat down over your board as you ride in order to let the lip pass over you, and cover you up—that is, break up and over you in a white, foamy little washdown with no significant force (Photo 7.19).
- **True tube ride.** The conditions are still small, but hollow with tubes developed enough to pass fully overhead if you are squatting low. You drop in, set up for a run along the wave face, stall, then pull in hard and get low. You can lean down and in toward the wall and grab your outer rail to keep the board tracking in tight to the wave base, preventing drift out toward the impact zone. You can do this frontside or backside, with the rail grab particularly helpful for pulling in on the latter. Welcome to the *green room* (Photo 7.20).

PHOTO 7.18 Getting started on tube riding with a head dip. You set this up, fundamentally, as you will your tube rides, positioning right at the pocket, in tight to the wave, bending down to get the feel of being under the lip as it starts to break.

PHOTO 7.19 Progressing to the little cover-up. Here again, position is at the pocket, and you are pulled in to a line of travel very nearly parallel with the wave crest and right up against the wave. You're getting started, remember, on small, not-so-hollow waves, so you need to squat way down in your stance to allow that lip to wash over the top of you as you keep speeding along (a, b). Maintain your balance so that you emerge from this experience triumphant and standing, shooting out onto unbroken wave face (c).

PHOTO 7.20 And finally, here's Joel Tudor showing that longboarders can get tube rides too. He performs an angled take-off appropriate to this sufficiently sizable and powerful wave and blisters along and down the wave face riding on the trim spot (a). This is a fast, top-to-bottom, hollow wave with a true tube, and Joel has taken off in precisely the correct position to be able to race down this glide path and have the pocket catch up to him and begin to envelope him in the tube. He makes all this possible by bending way down, since this is not a very large wave (b, c). Staying deeply crouched, Joel stays *in the shade* for a good bit of time (d, e), and then shoots out the end of the tube section just as it collapses behind him, straightening up out of the deep crouch and celebrating with a clenched fist (f). What a feeling!

(continued)

Making the Wave

Imagine you're out surfing a beach break on a day with a variety of different-sized peaks coming in to an assortment of different sandbars and shallow areas, distributing variously equipped and skilled surfers around the vicinity. As you watch, one surfer will take off, start riding, and get closed out, maybe resigning to turning off in front of whitewater to finish. The next surfer will take off on an identical-looking wave, keep translating the ride into additional sections, and finally kick out way down the line after a long and spectacular experience. That surfer *made the wave*. The first one didn't.

Making the wave means employing your bag of techniques to varying incoming swells to successfully negotiate your way along the surfable length of the wave as it breaks sequentially and finally expends the last of its energy. The faster and steeper the wave, the faster you need to get the things done that will enable you to maintain the continuity of your ride. There are three main ways to do it, and the essence of all of them is developing and maintaining board speed.

- **Explosive second turn.** You fade turn, or bottom turn off a straight or angled take-off, then carry this speed up the wave face and add to it with the second trip down the wave face off this second turn.
- **Direct to trim spot.** Instead of forcing it, you let gravity and wave power do the work for you, by executing whatever take-off you choose and then positioning yourself optimally in the wave face and establishing perfect trim. This is a finesse approach and is more traditional.
- **Pumping and driving.** You stay flat-footed and aft on your board and drive hard through a series of short turns, using the back portions of your rails and back foot pressure on the fins to pump increasing speed and power into the run by force. This is a progressive longboarder and shortboarder approach.

Look back over the photo sequences in this chapter, and you will see situations where it pays to perform delaying maneuvers—where it's possible to perform top turns, bottom turns, cutbacks, reentries, and floaters, and still make the wave. In other situations, making the wave means getting on a speed track and in trim and running along as fast as you can. This is usually the case with the biggest, most powerful waves—you drop in on an angle and run for your life, no fooling around. The things you choose to do start with the surf spot you select, your equipment preference, and how you enjoy riding. Some of the things people are doing on surfboards these days to entertain themselves are truly amazing.

High-Performance Maneuvers

Two premier high-performance maneuvers are the 360-degree turn and the 360-degree aerials, both helicopter and somersault varieties. The aerials are shortboard performances, while the turns can be executed on either longboards or shortboards. In the case of longboards, one can do either a nose 360 or a tail 360, whereas on shortboards the 360 turns are made from the tail. A tail 360 is more difficult to pull off on a longboard than on a shortboard, a point made, with a smile, by longboard master Dino Miranda to Wingnut one afternoon in Hawaii. In effect: "One of the younger surfers came up to me and asked how it was possible to do a tail 360 on a longboard, and I told him go practice it on your shortboard, and when you get that down I'll show you how to do it on a longboard."

On a longboard, both a nose 360 and a tail 360 depend on what is in essence an equipment failure to succeed, putting the board into a position so that the tail can no longer hold on to the water, so it pops out and releases, allowing the surfer to spin the board around, then force the tail back in and continue. Wingnut started doing nose 360s by improvising on an accident. When putting weight on the nose while angling down a small wave with a spilling crest, the tail pops out, then starts getting pushed into rotation by the whitewater of the wave crest. Wingnut leans into and applies foot pressure in the direction of the rotation, all the while sliding forward on the crumbled, gentle wave face, completing the turn by hopping back on the tail and pressing down until the nose is again pointing into the original direction, then he quickly gets back into trim position and straightens to stand (Photo 7.21 shows Joel Tudor doing the same maneuver). This maneuver can be performed off a nose ride on more powerful waves as well.

The tail 360 is a little different in that the surfer gets the weight back and throws the board up on the lip of a small wave just about to crumble from the top, then immediately gets his or her weight forward on the nose, releasing the tail, swinging it around 90 degrees so that the fins then hit and bite into the lip of the wave. The surfer then shifts weight back to raise the nose and spin it the rest of the way around and onto the original course. See *Endless Summer II* for the nose 360 by Wingnut, the section filmed in Costa Rica, and *Wingnut's Art of Longboarding 3: The Quest for Style* for the tail 360 by Dino Miranda. Shortboard 360s are initiated also by driving off of the tail and have become commonplace these days. See Kelly Slater performing one on a good-sized wave at Cloud Break in the Fiji portion of *Endless Summer II* back in the days when it wasn't so common.

Aerial maneuvers are another relatively recent development, an extension, if you will, of the reentry. Aerial surfing first came on the scene

PHOTO 7.21 Joel Tudor begins a nose 360, improbably, by rocketing along high in a reasonably powerful wave on a nose ride (a). Suddenly he leans sharply into the wave, knees bent, weight on the balls of his feet, driving the nose right into the lip, which pops the tail clear of the water (b), freeing resistance so that the rotational momentum Joel has applied to the nose can begin swinging the tail around (c). Joel sinks the nose and keeps leaning into the turn, pressing through the balls of his feet (d). With the tail clear, the forward motion of the wave pushes the nose the rest of the way around, and Joel responds by getting his weight back over the centerline and shifting back toward the tail (e). The board is level and Joel is nearly back to the middle, his position and weight the pivot point of the swinging board (f). He gets back toward the tail and completes the turn with back foot pressure, then begins to accelerate on the wave again in riding position (g).

(continued)

in the late 1970s, gained a burst of exposure and momentum from the work of Californian Christian Fletcher in the late 1980s, and by the mid-1990s had been added to the repertoires of many top pros. Taj Burrows of Western Australia would certainly be considered one of the carriers of the torch, and you can see some of his early work in this area on the DVD *Step into Liquid*. These maneuvers are often based on driving hard up wave faces and following through whatever momentum has been purposely imparted by the power and trajectory of the launch, then reaching down to hold the board, skateboard-style, to land it. Laird Hamilton certainly inspired some of this with his amazing launches into complete somersaults off wave crests at the end of tow-in rides on the enormous ocean swells piling into a location nicknamed "Jaws" near Maui, Hawaii (see the DVDs *Endless Summer II*, *Step into Liquid*, and *Laird*). Now some surfers have attached foot straps to regular shortboards so they can paddle on to hollow reef waves, drop in steeply and develop maximum speed by driving off one or more turns, then launch airborne off the inner curvature of the lip to complete spiraling somersaults. Go to worldsurfaris. com and request their promotional DVD on Pohnpei, Caroline Islands, in Micronesia, for some excellent footage of this maneuver, as well as some stunning tube rides in a location few have ever surfed.

Look how far you've come now, from wobbling up on your first waves to reading about and viewing things like launching skyward off sixty-foot wave faces. It's high time we go shopping and cull and refine from the enormous array of equipment out there a few boards that will greatly enhance the fun you can have surfing.

Surfboards and Accessories

The purpose of this book, remember, is to provide you with a unique distillation of highly relevant information that will jump-start and sustain your successful conquest of surfing, in a manner that we feel would have helped us enormously had it been available earlier. We intend for this book to be the main tool you use to carry through the feeling you have after watching *Endless Summer* and *Endless Summer II*. What do you do about that glow? How can you nurture and feed that ember and transform it into a steady, strong flame that burns the rest of your life?

The first step is to reemphasize how we define that term *success*: having fun. This definition means you can start genuinely experiencing success on your first day out. This doesn't have to be some arduous and painful mountain you must climb, with all of the rewards stacked at the end. The key is applying the right perspective, with the right gear, to the right wave.

Go to any of the major surf gear manufacturers' websites, and you may find the volume and complexity of what is available out there bewildering. It's easy to forget that the sole material requirement to go surfing is one surfboard. You don't even have to buy it. You can borrow or rent. It's almost always quite helpful these days to also acquire a leash and, although you can surf naked, a swimsuit or board shorts. If the water's cold, you'll need a wetsuit—and that's really it.

Therefore an encyclopedic, or even reasonably comprehensive, presentation of four million different surfboards and a plethora of accessories in this chapter wouldn't help you one bit. That's what the Internet is for. What *will* help you, immensely, is to refine and extract for you, out of this morass of information, a subset of highly applicable principles and recommended boards and accessories that you can count on, a sure-fire pathway to success. It doesn't matter that there are many other possibilities—there's lots of ways to go about it. What does matter is that you can be sure this chapter will work for you.

Historical Perspective

To truly understand where you are going, you need to have at least an inkling of where you've been. Search the Internet for "history of surfing" and you will see article after article about Polynesian origins; the eventual spread to California and soon after Australia in the early 1900s; and the synergistic timeline of landmark names, waves, locations, media events, and technological breakthroughs that have defined the nearly 100-year modern history of the sport. The current worldwide embrace of old-fashioned, paddle-on-the-wave surfing is truly a phenomenon. Other board sports wax and wane, but in the past forty years surfing has gone off the scale. Why?

A white guy, apparently the first human to attempt putting this into written words, comprehended the answer to this question. Lieutenant James King, in 1779, newly anointed commander of the *Discovery* after Captain James Cook ended up on a cooking fire, obviously understood— way back then—that surfing for Hawaiians entailed a deep-seated spirituality and unique, very powerful appeal connected with their skillful rides. These characteristics have continued to drive human beings of all ages, genders, colors, sizes, and ethnic and national origins to surf. Give them the slightest exposure to it, the smallest opportunity, and a very high percentage of them will feel compelled to try it. Give them the tiniest taste of success, and they're hooked. They're never the same again. For the more seriously afflicted, life trajectories change, influenced to varying degrees by surfing. This is the single most cogent factor, or take-home lesson, we derive from the history of surfing. It's the very reason you are reading these words, the reason so many of you will read this chapter and then spend your money on surfing equipment. We're here to make sure this won't be a fruitless exercise in "retail therapy."

Development of the Modern Surfboard

Literally hundreds of years ago, master Hawaiian craftsmen were splitting koa tree logs and lovingly shaping them with adzes and coral blocks, rough-sanding with sand, and wet-sanding with shark skin the mahogany-like material to produce beautiful solid-wood longboards fundamentally similar to modern surfboards. They were also producing the ancient precursors to the boogie board. The spirituality and passion driving these earliest surfboard shapers and their clients can't be much different from exactly what is occurring today. Today's shapers and surfers are inescapably connected by this passion all the way back to those earliest Polynesian pioneers. These original surfers had lovely boards too, and they surfed them very skillfully in some very challenging conditions, centuries ago, long before the first European-derived person was even aware of the sport, much less actually trying it.

Unfortunately, like nearly every other island society in the vast area of Pacific islands collectively termed Oceania, their eventual contact with Europeans was disastrous. The indigenous population of Hawaii had dwindled from perhaps as high as 800,000 in 1778 when Captain Cook "discovered" the island chain, to about 40,000 by 1896. Surfing was central to the culture of the thriving society Cook encountered. As with the people and society, however, it fell victim to the same sequence of events repeated throughout the region: missionaries establishing a beachhead, paving the way for traders and slavers, followed by catastrophic mortality of locals (and their culture) from subsequent conflicts, disease, and religious pressure, resulting in an altered, suppressed, "converted" remnant of a former society that then gets usurped or annexed by a foreign power. A photo preserved in Honolulu's Bishop Museum Archive, taken around 1890, of a Hawaiian standing on the beach with his board (possibly the first photo of a surfer), is truly a tribute to the indomitable spirit of surfing. Surfers at this time were teetering on the brink of extinction, with only a few isolated pockets of them left, all Polynesians, including a few at surf spots on Oahu, Kauai, and Maui (and to a lesser extent at other outliers like Tahiti).

In a strange twist of fate several descendants from the societies that virtually destroyed surfing were largely responsible for initiating the process of bringing it back to life. Although scattered reports exist of visiting Hawaiians surfing in California between 1835 and 1885, some on solid redwood boards they shaped from local trees, it's fair to say that Jack London's 1907 sojourn to Hawaii and resulting magazine article "A Royal Sport: Surfing in Waikiki" marked the beginning of the modern-day comeback of surfing. Two white guys hanging out in Hawaii surfing at the time, Alexander Ford and George Freeth, were inspirational for London. The first real explosion of interest, however, resulted from the early exploits and public surfing demonstrations of Hawaiian Duke Paoa Kahanamoku in California (1912) and Australia (1915), all on solid wood surfboards shaped from local materials. When Duke shaped and surfed an 8′6″ Hawaiian *alaia* out of local pine in the latter demonstration, he ignited the imagination of an entire young nation that would much later contribute heavily to the development of the shortboard. The synergism between Hawaii, California, and Australia established so early in the modern era of surfing continues to this day.

Was Duke's 8′6″ the first shortboard? It fits the definition of less than three feet greater than his height. George Freeth began reducing board length too, shaping and riding solid redwood boards down to 6′ in California before 1920. Nonetheless, shortboards didn't well and truly come on the scene until the 1960s and early 1970s, rising on a foundation of many technological developments, beginning with the construction of the first hollow board (in 1926) and the invention of the surfboard fin (1935), both by Tom Blake. In between, the popularity of his designs supported the first commercial production surfboards (by 1930). Meanwhile the use of balsa wood mainly from Ecuador (1932) cut board weight by almost two-thirds (from an average of about 100 pounds to about 35 pounds), and shapers in Hawaii by 1934 had eliminated the full square tail and modified the rails to promote maneuverability. Pete Peterson built the first fiberglass board, hollow with a redwood stringer (1946), and Bob Simmons in 1949 produced the first foam-core fiberglass board, the precursor, it's fair to say, of today's surfboards.

The 1950s saw improvements in fiberglassing techniques, a reduction in average board length to about 9′6″, and finally the first commercially successful fiberglass on polyurethane foam surfboard by Hobie Alter in 1958. Shapers Joe Quigg and Matt Kivlin improved the tail refinements and other modifications initiated in the 1930s by the Hawaii crowd, and Dale Velzy and his apprentice, Hap Jacobs, built on this foundation with great commercial success in California. Pioneering surfers led by the likes of Rabbit Kekai, Wally Froiseth, John Kelly, and Woody Brown were by this time taking on bigger and bigger waves in Hawaii, pushing the increasingly modern materials and designs to the max. One of the single most pivotal events drawing masses of Californian surfers and their new boards to Hawaii was a famous 1953 photo of Woody Brown and two other madmen (Buzzy Trent and George Downing) dropping in on an enormous wave at Makaha, Oahu. Another huge splash was the introduction of the cutting-edge fiberglass-and-balsa Malibu longboard to Australia by a group of Californians in 1956. Jack O'Neill created the first wetsuit in the early part of this decade, and it was in full production at Santa Cruz, California, by 1959, the same year that the earliest *pop-out*, or molded surfboard, came out (two successful examples being those by Dave Sweet and Chuck Foss).

While average board length dropped to just under 10′ in the 1950s, the mid-1960s to early 1970s saw it drop to about 6′. Dick Brewer designed an early prototype, featuring twin fins, intended to ride deep in the pocket, followed by Sam, a shortboard designed by Bob McTavish and George Greenough and popularized when fellow Australian Nat Young rode it to win the 1966 World Championships. By 1967 Clark Foam was mass-producing lightweight, high-quality polyurethane surfboard blanks that would supply the majority of the market for the next thirty-five years. Removable fin systems, a wide variety of tail shapes, and other design modifications, as well as the board leash (in 1971), revolutionized surfing and firmly entrenched the shortboard as the dominant choice for up-and-coming surfers. Nearly all commercially successful surfboards were fiberglass on individually hand-shaped polyurethane foam blanks with a wood stringer or stringers (internal lengthwise wood strips) for added stiffness. Significantly, however, the late 1960s saw more development of pop-out technology—producing stringerless surfboards in fixed molds—including the introduction of epoxy resin in place of polyester resin, and by 1970 the first use of polystyrene blanks by European windsurfer manufacturers beginning to use this process. Australians were also doing some pop-out innovations in the 1970s.

Surf historians credit an Australian named Simon Andersen with designing in 1981 the *thruster*, the triangular arrangement of three same-sized fins that remains the standard for most shortboards and some longboards today. Also by the early 1980s, pop-out technology using epoxy resin on polystyrene blanks for windsurfing board production had become the standard in Europe. "Conventional" surfboard construction continued to be predominantly polyester resin fiberglassing on hand-shaped polyurethane blanks with a wood stringer or stringers. During the 1990s commercially successful epoxy/polystyrene pop-out surfboards became established in the United States and began to compete with custom conventional surfboards, helped by greater strength and lighter weight. On shapes, longboards made a big comeback and were firmly reestablished by 1995, helped in no small way by Wingnut's exploits in *Endless Summer II*. Shortboards, guns, and other intermediate boards remained at least as popular, and pop-out *softtops* and other foam boards became extremely popular with beginners, with kids, and for use by the growing number of surf schools. In the 2000s, the fish shortboard has really come into its own (despite first appearing in 1967), with its swallow or fish tail, softer rails, less rocker, and greater width and thickness granting access to a shortboarding experience in smaller, weaker surf and, because of easier wave catching and more forgiving riding characteristics, to less experienced, less skilled, and aging surfers.

Surfboard Characteristics and What They Mean for You

Our examination of two different longboards in Chapter 4, centered around Figure 4.2, introduced many of the fundamental characteristics of surfboards in general—planshape or outline, thickness, length and width, nose and tail, rocker and rails—and what they can do for you. Let's expand that discussion now to encompass the full range of modern-day boards, and add to our knowledge a discussion of the effects of foil, different fin arrangements, bottom contours, and other details, none more important than the tail.

Take a look at Figures 8.1, 8.2, and 8.3, depicting a selection of surfboards that cover the spectrum of modern design, a collection that would actually constitute a superb quiver (surfboard array) for any enthusiast who is up and riding and ready to plunge in with both feet. The details of these views, dimensions, and captions, taken as a sequence—longboard-funboard-gun-shortboard-fish—tell a story. You'll want to refer to these figures during our discussions of specific board characteristics.

- **Planshape, length, thickness, width, nose, and tail.** As we traverse from the Wingnut longboards (Figure 8.1) through the intermediate boards (Figure 8.2) to the Byrne Easy Rider shortboard (Figure 8.3), planshape goes from a rounded, elongated outline with wide nose and tail to a squat, pointy, narrow-nosed outline. Length, width, and thickness decrease. The nose and tail width decrease. Hull speed decreases, while maneuverability increases.
- **Foil.** Foil is the longitudinal flow of thickness of the surfboard through the front (nose), middle, and back (tail) thirds, determined by the shaping of the blank. Thicker noses support forward trim and overall stability; thinner noses are more maneuverable. The middle third supports the chest and must adequately buoy the prone, paddling surfer. Thicker middles and tails make the board paddle better, catch waves more easily, and maintain better speed in smaller, weaker surf by preventing the board from submerging, which increases drag.
- **Rails.** The edges of the cross-sectional foil of a surfboard are called rails. Figure 4.2 introduced hard and soft rails. Figure 8.4 includes two more rail types, the chine and the tucked-under edge. In order of increasing tendency to shed or release water, rail types include soft, chine, tucked-under edge, and hard. The bigger and steeper the wave, the harder the rail so it cuts in and holds at high speeds; the smaller

FIGURE 8.1 Longboards revisited—Wingnut's favorite two boards.

Robert August Wingnut 2 (W2)				**Robert August Wingnut Noserider**		
Length:	9′	274.32 cm		Length:	9′4″	284.48 cm
Nose:	16.75″	42.54 cm		Nose:	19″	48.26 cm
Mid:	22″	55.88 cm		Mid:	23.75″	58.42 cm
Tail:	13.5″	34.29 cm		Tail:	14.5″	35.56 cm
Thick:	3″	7.62 cm		Thick:	3″	7.62 cm
Volume:	63 cc			Volume:	75 cc	
Fins:	Surf 10″			Fins:	Surf 10″	
Technology:	Tuflite			Technology:	Tuflite	
	(By Surftech)				*(By Surftech)*	

Both of these boards were designed by Wingnut and legendary surfer/shaper Mark Martinson. Both feature reduced nose kick (flatter forward rocker), a 10″ single fin, and square tail. While the single fin is "looser" for turns and more forgiving for nose-riding balance adjustments, both the flat entry and square tail enhance wave catching. This tail also confers harder turning capability than smaller-area tails. The narrower planshape (mid, tail, and nose) and thinner rails of the W2 allow it to handle larger surf. The Noserider is a modernized 1960s design, a bigger, broader board featuring a very wide nose with a flat planing bottom contour, and a bit more tail rocker. The rails are soft back through the tail, so that rather than releasing, the water flowing aft wraps right around the rounded rails, due to uninterrupted surface tension, and covers the tail, helping to hold it in while you are camped out having a cup of coffee on the nose. If Wingnut could only have one board, it would be the more generalized W2, which also nose rides well. However, his second board would be the Noserider.

Ariel Medel

WINGNUT'S COMPLETE SURFING

FIGURE 8.2 Excellent midsized transition boards, a funboard (Robert August 8′ Hyper Fun) and a gun (Wayne Lynch 7′6″ Freeform).

Robert August Hyper Fun

Length:	8′	243.84 cm
Nose:	11.75″	27.94 cm
Mid:	20″	50.80 cm
Tail:	14.5″	35.56 cm
Thick:	2.875″	5.08 cm
Volume:		55.5 cc
Fins:	FCS	2 and 1
Technology:	Tuflite	

(By Surftech)

Wayne Lynch Freeform

Length:	7′6″	228.50 cm
Nose:	12.25″	30.48 cm
Mid:	21″	53.34 cm
Tail:	14.125″	35.56
Thick:	2.4375″	5.08 cm
Volume:		48 cc
Fins:	FCS	Thruster
Technology:	Tuflite	

(By Surftech)

The Robert August 8′ Hyper Fun is your next step down in size from a longboard. This board catches waves well and is easy to ride. With flat rocker and plenty of volume and width in the nose, it has "edgy" as opposed to soft rails, and the tail features wings to both increase tail width further aft and shorten the length of the rails, utilizing a swallow tail, all combining to make the board looser (more maneuverable, easier) to turn. This is a new, modernized rendition of a fundamental "full-sized fun board" design that has been very successful for some thirty years. You could also class it as a "full-sized fish." This design is not intended for larger waves. It's a big, fun, loose-turning board perfect for smaller, weaker surf. This board will break out, skitter, and have control problems on big wave faces. The Wayne Lynch 7′6″ Freeform is your next step toward shortboard skills, and it will not have the control problems on bigger, more powerful waves because of its increased rocker and reduced thickness, volume, and tail width compared to the Hyper Fun. The rounded pin tail design is tighter (not as easy to maneuver but more suitable for larger waves), smooth-turning, and holds in well, and combined with the wider, softer planshape curves and high volume, this board paddles well and has good drive, speed, and tube-riding characteristics. It's a bit of a stretch to call it a gun—guns are typically narrower overall and in the nose and tail—it's a big, stable yet maneuverable and versatile full-sized shortboard.

Ariel Medel

FIGURE 8.3 Two easy-to-ride shortboards.

Byrne Easy Rider				Surftech Soul Fish		
Length:	6′8″	203.20 cm		Length:	6′6″	198.12 cm
Nose:	11.75″	29.84 cm		Nose:	15.375″	39.05 cm
Mid:	19.75″	50.16 cm		Mid:	21″	53.34 cm
Tail:	14.5″	36.83 cm		Tail:	15.375″	39.05 cm
Thick:	2.75″	6.98 cm		Thick:	2.5″	6.35 cm
Volume:	42 cc			Volume:	39 cc	
Fins:	FCS Thruster			Fins:	Future Thruster	
Technology:	Tuflite			Technology:	Tuflite	
	(By Surftech)				*(By Surftech)*	

The Byrne 6′8″ Easy Rider is, by shortboard standards, wide, thick, and stable, suitable for beginners and for heavier, older riders to 220 pounds. This board paddles well and is easy to ride, yet the large area conferred by its squash tail, and the slightly concave vee bottom, make it responsive and allow you to carve sharp turns, handling intermediate between loose and tight. It has pronounced rocker and will perform well in up to six-foot waves. The Surftech 6′6″ Soul Fish, on the other hand, is significantly wider, has more width and volume in the nose and tail, and has very little rocker for a flat entry and exit (small nose and tail kick), making it a great paddler and wave catcher, and it will run well through flatter wave sections. The soft rails are forgiving and in combination with the loose-turning fish tail ensure smooth, easy turning. This board is designed to maximize your fun in weak and small surf to shoulder height. It's very easy to ride and maneuver. It also comes in a 6′ and 6′10″ depending on your size (the latter will work for older riders to about 225 pounds).

Ariel Medel

the wave, the softer the rail, for more forgiving, smoother, drawn-out turning. Most shapers vary the rail considerably along the length of the board, and generally make them harder further aft. All the rails in Figure 8.4 are *down under* in that the apex of the curvature is past the

FIGURE 8.4 The shape, in cross section, of the edge or rail of your surfboard controls the degree to which water releases from it as it moves on a plane during a ride.

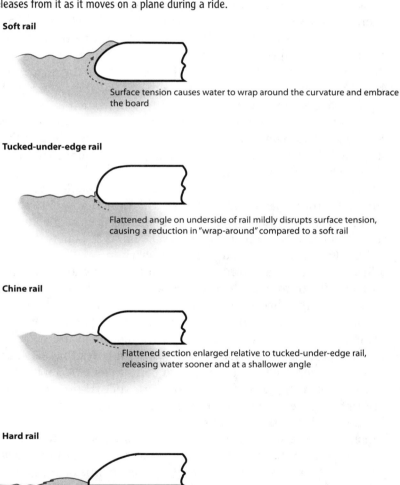

Soft rail

Surface tension causes water to wrap around the curvature and embrace the board

Tucked-under-edge rail

Flattened angle on underside of rail mildly disrupts surface tension, causing a reduction in "wrap-around" compared to a soft rail

Chine rail

Flattened section enlarged relative to tucked-under-edge rail, releasing water sooner and at a shallower angle

Hard rail

Water releases abruptly straight out (horizontally) from the rail

Increasing tendency to release water

midpoint going from deck to bottom. Manufacturers also describe rail characteristics in terms of proportion of curvature above and below this apex, for example, $^{50}/_{50}$ rails (soft, forgiving, less speed and performance). The soft rail in Figure 8.4 is approximately $^{60}/_{40}$.

~ **Rocker.** The longitudinal curvature of the bottom of the board increases substantially going from Wingnut's longboards to our sample shortboard, the Byrne Easy Rider. Less (flatter) rocker paddles more easily, catches waves more readily, and turns more drawn out (less responsive or *tighter* to turn). Greater (more curved) rocker is more responsive (*looser* turning) and will turn much more sharply, and of course it's more resistant to pearling (sticking the nose) when taking off on steeper wave faces.

~ **Bottom contours.** Like the rails, the norm is for the shape of the board's bottom, viewed in cross section, to vary along the length of the board. Bottom contour controls water flow, which in turn affects speed. Figure 8.5 shows a sample of bottom contours used in modern surfboards with comments on their intended effect. See also Figure 4.2 and Figures 8.1, 8.2, and 8.3 for examples of bottom contour influence on board performance.

~ **Tails.** The area of the tail, more than any other single factor, determines whether a particular surfboard will be more responsive (loose) or less responsive (tight) to turn and maneuver. Figure 8.6 illustrates a selection of tails and their influences. Examine the tail trends in our quiver (Figures 8.1, 8.2, and 8.3) for comparison.

~ **Fins.** Surfboards had no fins for several hundred years, then mostly just one fin from 1935 to the 1960s. Single and twin fins largely gave way to the thruster only in the early 1980s, except in the case of longboards, where either the single fin or the two-and-one tri-fin arrangement reigns. Wingnut and other top longboarders still use single fins, usually removable fins fixed in fin boxes that also permit adjustment fore and aft, to maximize performance flexibility. Single fins are more responsive to turning (looser), while tri-fin arrangements are tighter or less sensitive to turning commands. The hard-driving progressive longboarders and shortboarders use three fins. More traditional longboarders often prefer single fins. Fins used to be glassed on permanently to the board. Today most boards feature removable fin systems. Surfers now often bring a variety of fins on a trip to alter board performance to match day-to-day conditions. Shortboarders will also change to different-sized fins for different conditions—bigger fins for bigger waves and vice versa. The assortment of fin types, arrangements, and characteristics, and what they can do for you, are detailed in Figure 8.7. Photo 8.1 shows a variety of fins and describes relationships among form, size, and function.

FIGURE 8.5 Bottom contours, like rails, change from nose to tail on most boards and affect speed and handling.

Convex Bottom Contours

Belly—imparts drag as it cleaves and forces water aside, gives board a tendency to easily tilt back and forth on thickened longitudinal axis; used properly, can confer control in large, fast surf. When used, usually only in forward third of board.

Vee—normally used for the middle and aft thirds of the board to permit more ready leaning and tighter turning, as the surfer drives and presses off the angled flat planes on either side of the vee.

Flat—flat bottoms offer the least water resistance, pop up, and skim on plane the most quickly and easily, and respond most readily to turning pressure (very loose). However, their light grip on the surface can cause them to come unglued on bigger, faster, larger wave faces and skip, slip, skitter, and slide.

Concave Bottom Contours

Concave—usually wider forward and tapering aft to capture, squeeze, and accelerate water, creating lift (see Figure 4.2 boards).

Tri-plane—adds a central vee down the middle of a concave, reducing lift and conferring more responsiveness to turning pressure compared to the concave.

Channeled—this form of concavity traps and directs water in straight jets down the bottom and out the tail, preventing or curtailing release by the rails. This contour is not as responsive (loose) as the tri-plane, but converts more energy of a turn into forward projection coming out of the turn.

Ariel Medel

SURFBOARDS AND ACCESSORIES

171

FIGURE 8.6 By and large, when you drive a surfboard, you do it from the tail. Pressure on the tail turns the board. How the tail responds to this pressure is the most elemental determinant of the maneuverability of your board. The term *loose* describes the more reactive, responsive boards, while *tight* boards are less sensitive to turning commands. Generally, the more tail area you have to work with, the more responsive the board.

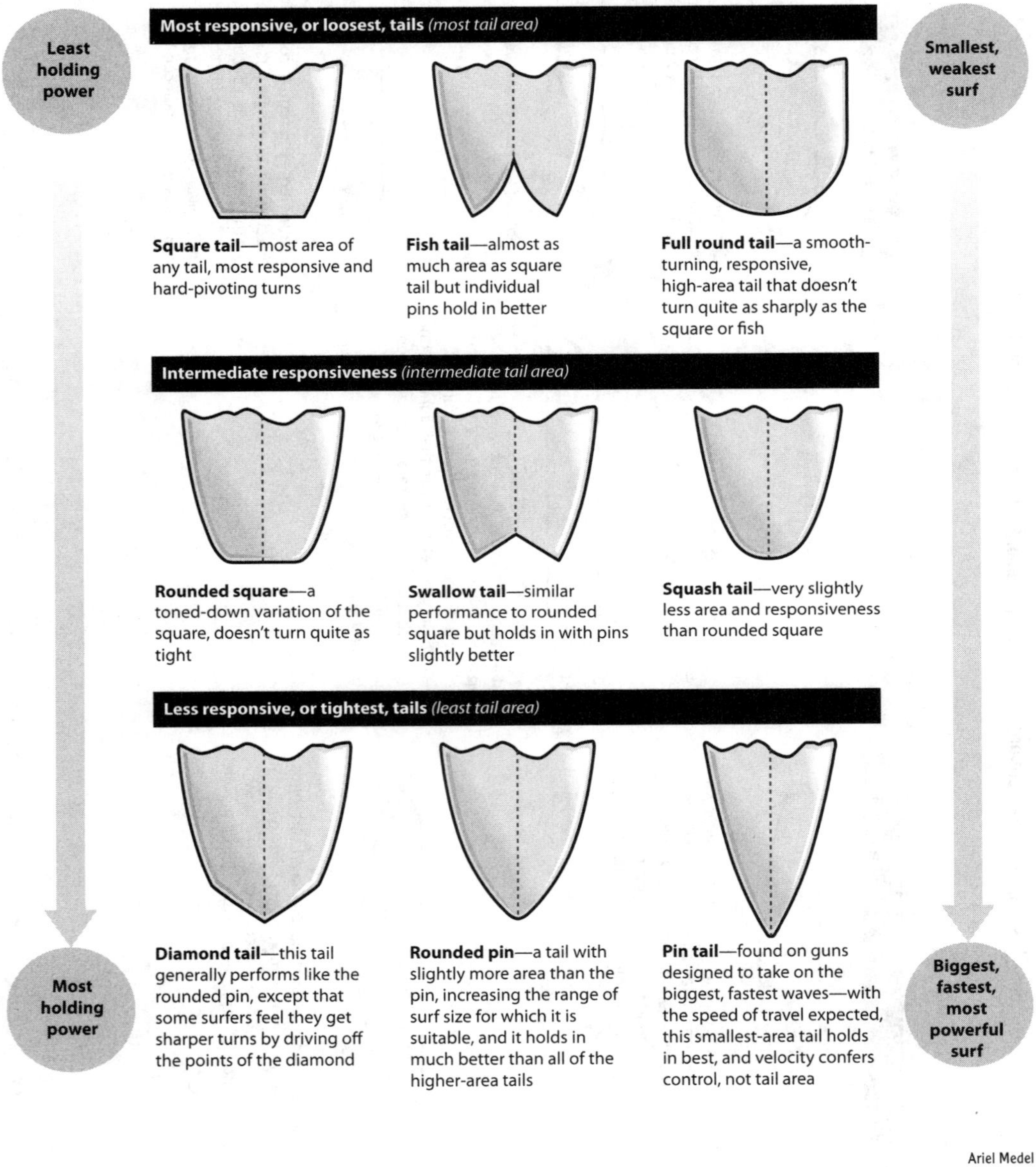

Least holding power

Smallest, weakest surf

Most responsive, or loosest, tails *(most tail area)*

Square tail—most area of any tail, most responsive and hard-pivoting turns

Fish tail—almost as much area as square tail but individual pins hold in better

Full round tail—a smooth-turning, responsive, high-area tail that doesn't turn quite as sharply as the square or fish

Intermediate responsiveness *(intermediate tail area)*

Rounded square—a toned-down variation of the square, doesn't turn quite as tight

Swallow tail—similar performance to rounded square but holds in with pins slightly better

Squash tail—very slightly less area and responsiveness than rounded square

Less responsive, or tightest, tails *(least tail area)*

Diamond tail—this tail generally performs like the rounded pin, except that some surfers feel they get sharper turns by driving off the points of the diamond

Rounded pin—a tail with slightly more area than the pin, increasing the range of surf size for which it is suitable, and it holds in much better than all of the higher-area tails

Pin tail—found on guns designed to take on the biggest, fastest waves—with the speed of travel expected, this smallest-area tail holds in best, and velocity confers control, not tail area

Most holding power

Biggest, fastest, most powerful surf

Ariel Medel

FIGURE 8.7 Everything you need to know about fin fundamentals.

Anatomy of a fin

Side view

Rake

Length

Base

Cross section

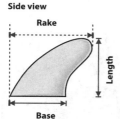

Symmetrical

Asymmetrical—used on side fins to promote holding power on wave faces, curved side always facing outboard

Force vector created from acceleration of water over greater distance of curved side relative to flat side (Venturi principle, like an airplane wing)

Fin arrangements (all fins shown can either be removable or permanently glassed on)

Modern standards

Single—fin position adjustable, forward for smaller waves (increased responsiveness to turning), aft for bigger, more powerful waves

2 and 1—single fin adjustable in fin box and symmetrical in cross section, side fins smaller, fixed in place by two stainless steel grub screws (Allen key supplied with new board), and asymmetrical

Thruster—the three-fin arrangement standard on most non-longboards. Back fin is symmetrical, side fins asymmetrical and curved side facing away from centerline

Modern, less common

Twin fin

Four fin

These arrangements are often seen on a fish planshape.

Fin angles

 = Force vectors resulting from water flowing past asymmetrical fins

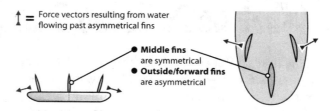

● **Middle fins** are symmetrical
● **Outside/forward fins** are asymmetrical

Outside/forward fins are usually angled outward to "loosen" the tail by creating slight lift. Reducing angle from vertical reduces this lift so the tail becomes less responsive and holds in better.

Outside/forward fins are angled leading end toward centerline to "loosen" the tail. This makes it more sensitive and sharper-turning. Turning them back away from the centerline "tightens" or stiffens tail response.

Ariel Medel

PHOTO 8.1 Fins come in all shapes and sizes. The more tail area in your board, the more fin area you need to control it, regardless of their number and arrangement. The longer and wider the fin, the better it will hold in and the less responsive the board will be to turning. The more rake, the less responsive and more drawn out the turns; the less rake, the more pivotal and responsive are the turns.

What to Do About Damage

The first scratches and dings (breaks in the integrity of the outer fiberglass skin of the board that allow water access to the interior foam) on one of your new surfboards are always among the most painful. Usually they're minor and are caused by physical contact—dropping your board on the rocks or parking lot, other handling and transportation trauma, getting in too shallow and hitting bottom in the process of a wipeout, or contact with another surfer's board. Occasionally major accidents occur, for example, another surfboard taking a major chunk out of your board in a collision, or a board snapped in half by the powerful impact zone of a wave. As your board ages, various signs of stress will eventually begin to appear: dents and cracks, fractures and shatters.

Much of the potential damage is preventable by protecting and handling your equipment properly and observing correct etiquette out in the surf. Inevitably, though, sooner or later you'll take your first casualty. It's important to look at your surfboard the way a sensible fisherman views a favorite lure. The good ones only last so long. They're used frequently, and they slowly get more banged up. Something catastrophic may happen that takes them away from you for good, or they eventually get so mangled that they have difficulty performing. The bright side is this means it's time to enjoy the excitement of getting a new lure, or a new board. In the meantime, don't sweat the damage. If it's serious, you can set that board aside, hop on another one, and head back out. Otherwise, temporary measures abound for repairing minor injuries so you can return to the playing field in very short order on the same board, and recent technology now provides us with superb kits that allow the repair of some fairly serious damage.

- **Board wax.** Minor dings can be temporarily sealed by rubbing a good load of wax into and over the spot, sealing it sufficiently to finish your surfing session.
- **Sealants.** Minor and more significant dings and cracks can be temporarily repaired by applying flexible adhesive/sealants that are both weatherproof and not prone to rapid deterioration from ultraviolet (UV) light exposure. Some products cure quickly so you can go back out; others, and for larger repairs, may require overnight curing.
- **Fiberglass and resin.** More permanent repairs were once the purview mostly of fiberglass tradesmen working in the surfing or other industries, and in the case of major damage still are. However, new, very complete repair kits are now available featuring UV curing resin that won't quickly yellow like some predecessors and that can be used on either polyester or epoxy surfboards.

Rather than muck you around with long-winded instructions that you will get in your repair kit anyway, let's get straight to the heart of the matter. We recommend the repair products of Surfco Hawaii, Inc. (surfcohawaii.com), specifically Rubberized Quick Fix (a sealant that will work for your wetsuit, surfboard, boogie board, fins, and other products), Quick Fix Putty (for strongly and permanently repairing polyester or epoxy surfboards in less than twenty-five minutes), and the All-Purpose Quick Fix Complete Kit (includes sandpaper, mixing sticks, UV curing resin, fiberglass roving and cloth, surfboard foam, scissors, and squeegee— unbelievable). The kit will handle repairs up to and including reglassing a permanent fin and fixing chunks taken out of your board down into the foam. You could actually be out surfing again within thirty to sixty minutes. Best of all, the materials of all of these kits are nonhazardous and airplane-safe.

A few words of wisdom on repair. Don't let dings go, or your interior foam will get waterlogged and ruined. Given the choice of a quick fix using a sealant versus using a permanent material, choose the latter. Then you're done. Since the first step of any repair is to remove materials from and sand out damaged spots, cured adhesive will only make this job more difficult later on. These new UV curing products are widely transportable, stable, and nonhazardous, all of the things that conventional fiberglassing supplies are not. Take them along, don't hesitate to follow the clear, simple instructions, and you'll be on your way. The other things these kits do is completely discredit the prevalent myth that there's some mystery to repairing epoxy resin boards (pop-outs)—the products work equally well on your custom-shaped polyester boards or your high-tech epoxy pop-out boards.

One last piece of advice: remember that your epoxy pop-out boards do not have stringers (the internal lengthwise wood strips used on custom-shaped, polyester-on-polyurethane-blank boards). So, if the integrity of the outer fiberglass skin is broken, say a big chunk taken out of a rail by another board's fin, you must fill in the foam, then use fiberglass cloth to refabricate the area of lost skin and overlap it with the undamaged surrounding skin to reestablish the longitudinal integrity of the board. Otherwise it may snap at the break in the skin.

The only thing we haven't covered here is the fact that your repair, if made on a painted section of your board, won't match. Keep surfing until you foresee a sufficient gap, then get the board to a professional repair facility. They'll match the paint, and seal the new spot with resin. Note also that this same facility can transform amazingly damaged boards into something that looks brand-new again.

Accessories for Surfing

While it's true that all you really need is a surfboard, Scott is just old enough to have experienced swimming repeatedly after a board with no leash and freezing because it wasn't worth buying a wetsuit for a brief surfing interlude with no idea when it would be possible to go again. That's a lot of time and energy wasted that could've been applied to surfing instead. He's also bald enough to appreciate other accessories like a surf hat. The difference between pursuing any intense, outdoor activity with a complete repertoire of the right equipment and underequipping or using the wrong gear makes an enormous difference in the enjoyment of the outing. Don't underestimate the value of picking out the right stuff. Let's go right down the list:

- **Leash.** Wingnut and his surfing buddies like to surf without a leash, conditions permitting. They're so good they can get away with it and not affect others. Nearly everyone else in most conditions will want to use a leash. Get a quality brand, about the length of your board, with a swivel at either end of the long, stretchy leash cord, attached to the ankle strap at one end and the flat piece of nylon strap on the other. This short strap section passes over the rail, between the string attachment cord and the leash cord. This is called the rail saver, because it prevents small-diameter cord from cutting into the rail under pressure (see Figure 2.3).

- **Wetsuit.** Hypothermia is dangerous and uncomfortable, and it prematurely ends outings. Wetsuits allow a thin layer of water to warm and seal next to the body. Top manufacturers produce an array of excellent-quality products. Finding a perfect fit is more important than specific brand, and different brands may tend to be smaller or larger in different dimensions for the same ostensible size. It's very important that the fit be snug, but not restrictive, particularly in the shoulders and across the back, which inhibits paddling. Prices vary widely depending on how fancy the material and accoutrements. The biggest names will have top-quality, nonleaking seam stitching and sealing, zippers, knee pads, thickened chest, and good flexibility. To be very specific, Scott has always had good luck with O'Neill, wearing a 3/2 millimeter Hammer model for ten years, and then getting a current rendition of exactly the same suit just last week since the original was literally falling off in pieces. The zipper had broken on his ten-year-old O'Neill 4/3 millimeter, and the local dealer said no problem; O'Neill's standard policy is to replace the zipper for a minimal fee and have the suit back to you within the week. When Scott went to pick up the repaired suit, O'Neill had said "no charge" (and they had no idea whatsoever about this book). How good is that? And the Hammer is nowhere near the top of their line—it's just a high-quality, reasonably priced wetsuit. Coincidentally Wingnut grew up near the company headquarters and wears O'Neill exclusively. On the other hand, Scott's son Ryan is on his second Quiksilver 3/2 and both have been superb. To find the suit for you, get on the Internet and look through the models. Consider what sorts of water temperatures they're designed to handle, decide on a thickness, go to the local dealer, kick the tires, and pick one out that fits perfectly. Be sure to take a plastic bag to place over your feet for ease of insertion and pulling up the legs of the suits you are trying on. Be patient and it will pay off.

- **Rash protection.** New ultrathin rash suits may permit being worn under your wetsuit, and if this is the plan, you'll want to buy the rash suit first, then try on wetsuits while wearing your rash suit and be darned careful that your shoulders and arms aren't restricted and binding when you paddle. The advantage is that even good-fitting wetsuits can rub you raw, around the armpits and neck, for example. Always have some Vaseline along to apply to these spots during a period of more intensive surfing. If you can find a newfangled rash suit to wear as an undergarment, why not? Otherwise, long- and short-sleeved rash tops, sans wetsuit, are popular in warmer waters for both UV protection and to prevent rashes developing on chest and abdominal areas in heavy contact with the waxy deck of your board while paddling.

~ **Head gear.** Billed surf caps are gaining in popularity. Models vary. All feature draw strings or chin straps to keep them secured. Shorter bills offer less water resistance and stay on better. The UV relief is superb. The other piece of head gear to consider is a helmet. Scott's son Ryan has a Gath; it fits perfectly and is very comfortable (gathsports.com). For dangerous reef breaks or any surfing area punctuated with rocks and other hard bottom, the wrong fall could be fatal. World champion Tom Carroll wore one at Cloud Break in Fiji for the filming of *Endless Summer II*. A helmet may give a beginning surfer just that margin of confidence to be comfortable at a point break. This was certainly the case with Ryan at ages four to seven. Now, at age nine, of course, he's more confident and too cool to wear it.

~ **Booties.** Here again, several top brands, including O'Neill and Rip Curl, produce excellent split-toe products for physical and thermal protection. Booties are a must for any reef break situation where there's any chance you'll do some walking across reef. They're also very handy for entering and exiting barnacle-covered rocky shorelines in more temperate climates. It's worth buying the purpose-built split-toes rather than trying to make full-foot dive booties work. The ability to flex the big toe separately makes all the difference for your surfing.

~ **Sunscreen.** Very few sunscreens seem to withstand the severe washing effect of surf. Zincs do the best, and in particular the stick formulations for lips are a must. Among creams and less pasty choices, try Bullfrog Surfer's Formula Gel (bullfrogsunblock.com).

~ **Goggles and sunglasses.** Purpose-built polarized surfing goggles or glass sunglasses are two possibilities for saving eyes from glare and UV damage while surfing. You see them occasionally, usually when conditions are small. The legendary Gerry Lopez may wear them the most of any luminary. Otherwise, it's fair to say it doesn't seem to have caught on, perhaps because most fear losing them during wipeouts or feel encumbered with the extra gear. The relief is substantial, however, especially at east-facing shorelines in morning hours. Impaired vision from salt deposits left by evaporating drops of seawater on the lenses is a disadvantage, and although dipping them helps, you are fiddling with gear instead of focusing on the surf.

~ **Webbed gloves.** Many waves are missed on very small margins of paddling effort. Webbed gloves therefore should result in that many more waves ridden. They do not seem to have caught on widely yet, despite being around for some time. Perhaps it's vanity. Perhaps it's the desire to minimize the amount of equipment worn and keep it simple. Why not give them a try? Kneeboarders always seem to wear them with good success.

~ **Traction pads.** This rubberized studded adhesive pad, often with a back raised ridge, is usually affixed near the tail on the deck, over the fins, for added back foot traction. They are used almost exclusively on shortboards. Available at any surf shop and popular with kids, they seem to work for many and so, why not? The flip side is if you don't feel a need for it, why bother? Just wax the board down and you should be fine.

~ **Nose guards.** Nose guards are protective adhesive sleeves for the nose area of surfboards, the spot most likely to be damaged—particularly from the popular young surfer's habit of slamming his or her shortboard into the sand nose first for vertical display in between surfing sessions at the beach. We'd say all those afflicted by that habit might want to consider nose guards.

~ **Board bag.** No point in buying a nice new board and then not protecting it. Single board bags come in different thicknesses of padding, depending on whether they are intended for local day use, road trips, or air travel. Most double and multiple board bags tend to come in thicker, air-travel configurations. Major brands generally deliver on quality, and one of the first places to look is the zipper. Undersized, cheap-looking zippers can corrode quickly and freeze, then break upon being forced. On the other hand, quality bags do a superb job through trying conditions. Scott bought two such bags made by FCS, and they survived a year at sea and another two years in a marina on the open deck of a sailboat, and they're still going strong to this day. He bought a thinner, cheaper brand two months ago for local use of another board, and the zipper has already frozen and broken off and the board already has one ding it got through the bag on a rough boat trip. Choose wisely.

~ **Waist pack.** A zippered, mesh bag fitted with a broad nylon strap that fastens with Velcro, these actually do not come off, even in heavy surf. Scott started out wearing one all the time, taking along small, light objects like lip zinc sticks, a bit of wax, a wax comb, car key on a string (handy also for securing a wedding ring that became very loose in cold water). Fellow surfers at one break kept requesting a coffee thermos. Eventually, it no longer seemed worth it or necessary, began to feel cumbersome, and he hasn't worn it for quite a while. If a situation arises on some trip where it's handy to have something along while you're out, this is a viable option.

The Final Decision

You've been through nearly everything you need to know to put it all together and launch, maintain, and build on your surfing success. What to do now? Go shopping. Go surfing. Get immersed.

There's just one thing we really need to discuss before you take the final plunges on boards. It's an issue we've nibbled around the edges of, and we need to take it full on here and now. In our discussion of surfboard development, we left you hanging a bit on what have emerged as the two main constructions as of this writing: custom-shaped polyester on polyurethane foam blanks and pop-out mold epoxy on polystyrene foam blanks. Which way should you go and why?

Essentially all of the professional shortboard surfers, and most of the professional longboarders, still surf custom polyester boards finely tuned to nuances so small that only a top pro could detect it. Nonetheless, an average, everyday person like you or Scott can go to a custom shaper, get weighed and measured, and if the shaper happens to have surfed alongside this client, he or she may have a good idea about skill level, physical condition, and personal goals. Any top shaper can then custom build a unique surfboard for you—as Robert August says, "That's *your* board, and there's not another one like it." And you will actually pay less for that board than you will an epoxy pop-out production board shaped by that same expert (basically because the construction materials for the latter are more expensive). Of course, on the other hand, every pop-out mold is the final result of thousands of hand-shaped surfboards by the experts engaged by epoxy board manufacturers—they don't just try expensive molds on speculation.

So why would anyone bother paying more for an epoxy pop-out—for example, the Tuflite technology used in the Surftech boards we've mentioned in this book? Well, they are lighter, stronger, and much more durable than polyester. They can take punishment that would (and often does) snap polyester in half. They tend not to dent, delaminate, or wither in tough outdoor conditions living in board bags on the decks of ocean-going vessels. They outlast most polyester boards by years. Scott's neighbor, an enthusiastic surfer now eighteen years old, has been through five custom polyester surfboards in three years (all snapped in half in heavy conditions). Scott over this same time has snapped one, an old polyester board, and surfed two of his epoxy boards since 2002, and they're still like new except for ding repairs—no dents, bumps, soft spots, shatters, stress cracks—and remember, they spent three years in bags on the deck of a sailboat crossing the Pacific and in Australia when they weren't in the surf. And they've been surfed a lot and hard (including traumatic experiences they wouldn't have gone through with a better surfer for an owner).

One major advantage of polyester is price. We discussed new custom boards, but if you're on a budget, the best deals in surfing are used polyester boards. Even the used epoxy boards are expensive. Not so with polyester. They can be dirt cheap. Have a good look at the condition, making sure to check for tail and nose damage, degree of permanent compressions of the glass and interior foam from hard use, around the fins and fin boxes for stress fractures, and for crazing and cracks perpendicular to the centerline, on both deck and bottom, indicating severe flexing that could have the board just about ready to snap in half. If you think it's got enough waves left in it for the price, what have you got to lose?

The other thing about polyester on polyurethane is the boards are a bit heavier. They have a different ride through the water, and a different sort of spring and response to pressure and drive, than the lighter, stiffer epoxy boards. On windy and rougher days, they may not be as subject to getting blown around and affected on wave faces as epoxy boards. But for most surfers, the lightness, durability, and strength of epoxy will serve them well. And like Wingnut says when asked about an array of new board technologies being tested (TL2, carbon fiber and graphite composites, Firewire, and so on), only about 1 percent of the surfing population can genuinely discern most of the performance margins . . . and Scott and most of the readers aren't in that 1 percent and never will be.

So what's the answer to the question? Either board technology, polyester or epoxy, would likely suit you fine. The most important thing is to get the right board for your size, weight, physical condition, wave conditions, and budget. And the only way you can do that is to resist being overwhelmed by all of the details, distill the decision variables down to the bare necessities of your surfing life, get on the Internet or to the surf shop, get off of some bucks, and walk out with your surfboard. So here's to you—good luck and enjoy yourself to the hilt.

Surfing for Everyone

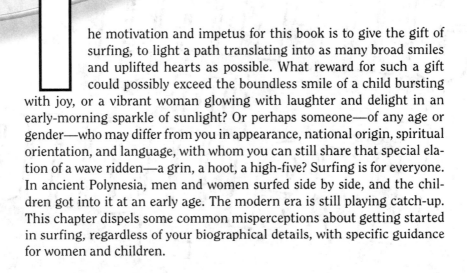

9

The motivation and impetus for this book is to give the gift of surfing, to light a path translating into as many broad smiles and uplifted hearts as possible. What reward for such a gift could possibly exceed the boundless smile of a child bursting with joy, or a vibrant woman glowing with laughter and delight in an early-morning sparkle of sunlight? Or perhaps someone—of any age or gender—who may differ from you in appearance, national origin, spiritual orientation, and language, with whom you can still share that special elation of a wave ridden—a grin, a hoot, a high-five? Surfing is for everyone. In ancient Polynesia, men and women surfed side by side, and the children got into it at an early age. The modern era is still playing catch-up. This chapter dispels some common misperceptions about getting started in surfing, regardless of your biographical details, with specific guidance for women and children.

Let's Start with the Kids

Even along coastlines popular for surfing, there seems to be this international myth that kids aren't ready to learn to surf until they are between the ages of about nine and twelve. This is absolutely false. Ryan and Cameron both started surfing before the age of three. Scott bought Ryan his first boogie board at age two (Photo 9.1) and his first fiberglass surfboard, a 5′2″ high-performance shortboard, at age three (Photo 9.2). Of course, that was a stupid move, as it was the wrong type of board, and it was fortunate that Ryan didn't get whacked in the head and put off of surfing as soon as they started messing around in some gentle spilling waves at Bargara, Queensland, Australia. Soon after, further south on the coast, Robbie Sherwell (Robbie Sherwell's XL Surfing Academy, robbie sherwell.com.au) corrected Scott when he and Ryan wandered near one of his classes, and he immediately loaned Ryan a 6′6″ foam longboard for nearshore whitewater work (Photo 9.3). Scott pushed his young son onto the small foaming waves washing over a shallow sandbar at low tide, and Ryan popped up and rode wavelet after wavelet all the way in to shore (he couldn't yet stand for more than a few seconds on the 5′2″, yet the floaty, more stable 6′6″ was no problem). He was beside himself, asking if

PHOTO 9.1 We started Ryan on a boogie board at age two. We found a tiny reef break washing up on a sandy little beach in American Samoa, pushed him on to the wavelets (a), and got him messing around with standing up (b, c). So far, so good.

Photos by Wendy Bannerot and Paea Tavake

PHOTO 9.2 About seven months later, for Ryan's third Christmas, Scott bought him a 5′2″ shortboard. Ryan opens this giant box aboard our forty-one-foot sloop *Elan* and is speechless (a–b). We set the board out on the aft settee and practice a few pop-ups right away (c–e). We're feeling really good now, ready for action (f). Next stop is Bargara Beach. Ryan waxes his new board for the first time (g), dons his new sun suit, grabs the board, and hits the waves (h). Scott leads him out by the nose of the board, and we await our first set (i). This one looks good—let's turn around, get into perfect trim, and get ready (j). Yes, it's perfect . . . a last check on the trim, and Scott pushes Ryan onto his first wave (k). Ryan is in perfect trim and ready to pop up as he glances back along the wave to see how it is developing (l). Whoops, this board is a little more tippy out here on a wave than it was back on the aft settee (m). Ryan doesn't pop up on the first one but he's still having fun (n).

Photos by Wendy Bannerot

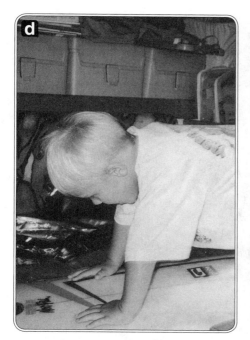

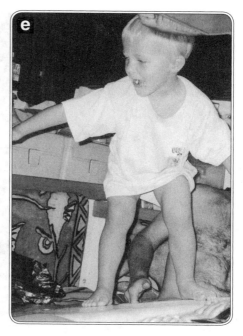

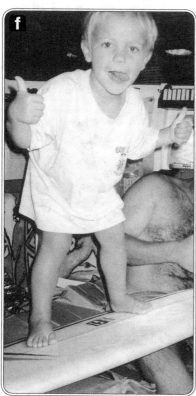

Photos by Wendy Bannerot

(continued) **187**

Photos by Wendy Bannerot

Photos by Wendy Bannerot

PHOTO 9.3 Ryan could never get up for more than a few moments on that tippy little 5′2″ in the early going. Further south on the coast we acquire what we should have bought in the first place, a 6′6″ foam board. We get out on a nice shallow sandbar at low tide, and just *look* at the massive difference the right wave and the right surfboard makes for Ryan. Scott tows him out by the nose of the board and we turn around and get ready in front of our first perfect whitewater wave (a). Scott pushes him on, the buoyant, stable 6′6″ catching the wave immediately, and Ryan, having now practiced his pop-ups for eight weeks, exhibits reasonable form (b), pops up easily and quickly, and is stand-up surfing with confidence at age three (c).

Photos by Wendy Bannerot

he looked "like Pat and Wingnut," to which Scott answered, "Maybe even better; you're doing an amazing job." They showed up for the entire week-long school, and Robbie lent them that board daily, refusing any money, finally caving in and selling them the board, even though his own supplies and ability to replace it were limited at the time. Ryan still has it, and it has been the entry door to the joy of surfing for many a youngster now nearly six years later, as well as the first board Ryan still wants to use for inaugural sessions in increasingly bigger surf.

So, the success formula for kids is quite straightforward:

~ **Their first boogie board.** Start children on a boogie board in very small sandy shore waves from age one and a half to two and a half. This gets them accustomed to feeling excited, happy, and stimulated in the surf, and bonds them tightly to the parent, who should of course stay right with them and ensure that they do not get caught in even a small shore dump that could throw them down hard enough to ruin the fun. Ryan, as we've seen, could handle some tiny reef wave situations and was standing up in minuscule conditions in American Samoa by age two and a half.

~ **Their first surfboard.** Buy kids their first foam surfboard at age two and a half to three. The 6′6″ or so length works really well for this age, and we highly recommend a leash (this way they're always connected to a "float" and it becomes a security feature). Have them practice pop-ups briefly at home or on the beach as a fun sort of game or challenge, maybe two to five times only per session out of deference to short attention spans, more if you can get them showing off and getting attention from relatives or competing with friends.

~ **Surf conditions.** Practice with a shallow, gradually sloping sand bottom, lower tide stages, whitewater sections only, on the smallest waves that will still push the board and rider. Water temperature should be warm and comfortable.

~ **Surf entry.** Have children lie prone on the board and tow them out by the nose of the board, lifting it above each oncoming wave, so they never get any wash, just tilt happily (wheeee!) and stay virtually dry the whole time. You've got them laughing and comfortable, and you're telling little jokes, making it all superfun. You do remind them always to fall flat or feetfirst, no headfirst dives off the board.

~ **Take-offs.** Choose the wave very carefully—nothing likely to rebreak or swell up at all. Hover over your minisurfers, grasping each rail firmly, and turn the board around, nose to beach. Double-check their trim, give a few soft words of encouragement, nothing that implies any pressure to perform ("OK, here you go, have fun!"). As the foaming little white crest reaches your position, push the board onto the wave. The final shove is usually right on the back of the tail.

~ **The ride.** Start out pushing them straight. Once they're confident, move over a bit on the bar and begin pushing them at a slight angle, and encourage them to continue it as a left or a right. Sooner or later this trajectory will carry them onto some unbroken wave face, which they'll then naturally seek since it's a faster and smoother ride—more fun! It's ideal to have a second parent, older child, or other adult waiting at the end of the ride in the early days, and there should be lots of cheering and encouragement, lots of positive reinforcement, regardless of the outcome. Scott will always remember Ryan on the way back out after one of his early falls, at age three, paraphrasing Bruce Brown's narrative from *Endless Summer II*: "No matter how long you've been surfing, a wipeout is *still* a wipeout." Within a few months, Ryan was getting eighty-yard rides at an ideal small beach break at just the right tide, actually attracting crowds, this tiny little three-and-a-half-year-old figure in a full sun suit zipping along ride after ride. We got Ryan's preschool classmates out, and on this foam board in these perfect conditions, they could do really well too, first time out. The take-home lesson? Give most any kid the right equipment and the right wave, and he or she can surf at age three, no problem. Why waste all of those years waiting to be nine?

~ **Coaching tips.** The surfer's stance should be head up, knees bent, feet angled across right on the centerline, back arm bent and up (a little higher than the front arm), front arm extended horizontally and in front, and over the centerline of the board. When the centerline moves laterally, the arm moves laterally, staying centered over it. Show kids they can get some drive and shock absorption by flexing their legs at the knees. Emphasize popping up to this position in perfect trim, and then either leaning to put weight forward, on the front foot ("stepping on the gas pedal"), or aft, on the back foot ("stepping on the brakes"). Nothing more for starters. They actually start to turn intuitively, alternately shifting weight to the balls of their feet or their heels, leaning forward and back, without any overload of further detailed instructions. Fundamentally, this is basic shortboarding—mostly standing in that one perfect spot, and doing everything with weight shifts and body movement.

~ **Teaching guidelines.** Never force it, never push. The moment they say "Let's go in and build a sand castle on the beach," readily agree, even if they've caught three perfect waves and the conditions are perfect for getting many more. Let them call the shots. Any day they indicate a preference for a boogie board, readily agree, and compliment them and aid them just as enthusiastically as if they were stand-up surfing. The other thing kids love about boogie boards is the independence—they can go out waist-deep and throw themselves onto their own waves, at their own pace, and get some great rides. Also, they'll often want to leave the boards on the beach and go swim freely in the waves with you, and body surf. This makes for excellent progress too—they learn to duck dive, either avoid or use rips, catch and ride waves, and feel confident through little hold-downs, all skills that will stand them in good stead later, all being acquired subconsciously while they frolic.

~ **Safety awareness.** Give kids a good coating of zinc sunscreen and a rash guard. You don't want the pain of sunburn to become associated with any part of the surfing experience. Keep them over sand, no rocks. Teach them about rip currents and always keeping cool. Never take your eyes off of them; stay as close to them as you can at all times. As you walk down toward the water, have a good look along the sand at the tide and wave marks for washed-up blue bottles, Portuguese man-o'-war, and other jellyfish, an indicator of what may be floating around, and cancel or move to another location if it looks likely that someone may be stung. While in the water, watch up wind, up wave, and up current for jellies and any other hazards, ready to get in between your children and the organism or take avoidance action. Keep a bottle of fresh water, vinegar, and a roll of paper towels on hand for first-line sting treatment. Always stay right with your children in the surf until take-off, and if at all possible have someone waiting at the arrival zone. Wetsuits and neoprene tops provide flotation in addition to warmth and protection from stings. It never hurts to surf near guarded beaches, conditions permitting. For very inexperienced and young kids, you'll want at least one adult per child in the water, specifically assigned to each other in pairs.

~ **Bring a friend.** It's impossible to overstate the power of synergism between similar-aged kids in the surf (Photo 9.4). A session that might last twenty minutes with Mom or Dad will turn into "surf until I drop" if a schoolmate or cousin is along and has a board to use. It could be as much as two hours of hard surfing, riding the same waves together, friendly competition—neither wants to be the first to quit. Foam boards easily allow towing two kids at a time (without damage since they don't ding if they bang together a bit), one in each hand, by the nose of the boards, spinning them around and then shoving them both on the same wave with a hand on the tail of each board. This situation also encourages them to gleefully paddle onto their own first waves rather than wait for Mom or Dad. Two hours of this is a real workout for the tow truck too, we can promise you.

~ **Moving up.** If you get your kids out surfing with any consistency, they progress rapidly. Ryan quickly acquired a skim board, his own new

PHOTO 9.4 Ryan and Connor Boland just after catching a bunch of fun waves. Notice that Connor is using Ryan's same old yellow foam 6′6″, one of many kids to get his start surfing on that great kid's learning board (Ryan by this time, age eight, is surfing a custom 5′6″ shortboard shaped by Peter "Stumpy" Wallace).

Photo by Matthew Bambling

boogie board, and began attempting to ride his 5′2″ more and more often in lieu of the 6′6″. This is when Scott took him to Peter "Stumpy" Wallace (stumpysurf.com) and had him measured for his first custom board (for his seventh birthday), a beautiful 5′6″ performance shortboard suited precisely to Ryan that glides and paddles and maneuvers to perfection for him. By that time he could ride the 5′2″, but his surfing increased exponentially having the right board. At age nine he still surfs this board and absolutely loves it.

Six months after Scott and Ryan got the 5′6″, it dawned on Dad that Ryan was missing a lot of days surfing because he owned only two shortboards, and his only longboard was foam, with performance limitations. He spoke to Stumpy about shaping Ryan a custom longboard that, for his size at age seven and a half, would be the precise equivalent of a 9′6″ for Scott. The result was an exquisite 7′2″ high-performance longboard for Ryan's seventh Christmas, and, once more, Ryan's surfing exploded into a whole new area of very long rides at a local point break, using trim and weight distribution to work his way across flat sections to steeper sections in a manner not possible on his shortboards; he was learning the beauty of surfing with less effort and less urgency (Photos 9.5 and 9.6).

No single act will enhance your children's surfing careers more than bestowing upon them the right surfboards, and this is one of the strongest possible arguments for visiting a local custom shaper for perfectly tailored polyester-on-polyurethane boards for your children. In particular, we very highly recommend getting your young enthusiasts both a shortboard and a longboard, and make sure they have a boogie board too. To be sure, they've got to earn it by showing the interest and commitment that this equipment will get the heck used out of it. Nonetheless, you are giving them much more than material toys; you are actually bestowing the spiritual gift of a lifetime, access to unbridled happiness through thick and thin. Scott spent a total of around $1,300 on those two custom boards for Ryan. They have Ryan's and Stumpy's names on them,

PHOTO 9.5 Ryan and Wingnut at Malfunction in Kingscliff, New South Wales, Australia, with Ryan's 5′6″ custom shortboard and his 7′2″ custom longboard, both shaped by Stumpy, and now signed by Wingnut for good luck.

Photo by Scott Bannerot

PHOTO 9.6 By the age of eight Ryan is an accomplished surfer, paddling on himself and popping up with practiced dexterity on a beach break (a) and executing a bottom turn as he sizes up the wave face developing to his right, with a slight check stall thrown in (b, c). He accelerates up in the wave face by changing his weight distribution for perfect trim (d, e), develops speed by dropping down the wave face (f), and translates this trajectory into maximum speed down the line to transit a steepening section (g, h). He stays pulled in as the section he is on collapses, and surfs right through the falls (i). He stays upright as the wave continues onward (j), then swings off and begins to drop back down prone to paddle back out to the take-off zone. That's an awful lot of fun for an eight-year-old, thanks to the right equipment and the right waves from an early age. Here's to more young girls and boys getting into it without delay!

Photos by Matthew Bambling

Photos by Matthew Bambling

(continued)

197

Photos by Matthew Bambling

and now they've even been signed in indelible ink by Wingnut. They're uniquely his boards. Two years later they're still going strong, having glided, with Ryan at the controls, over a combined total of more than two thousand waves. They've got lots of life left in them—years. While the

initial investment was substantial, the payback has been immeasurable, the original cost rendered inconsequential.

Wingnut and Cameron are of course in a different category (Photo 9.7). Cameron's dad is one of the best surfers in the world, an example of a well-deserved, pervasive celebrity status that has permeated surfing communities all over the globe. That's potentially intimidating to a ten-year-old contemplating taking up the same sport as Dad. Dad's a superstar. Comparisons and comments, however good the intentions, are inevitable and could easily feel like pressure. Consequently Wingnut is extra careful not to push Cameron. He stands way back and lets Cameron come to him in the area of surfing. And it has worked—Cameron is an excellent young surfer, although he tells Wingnut, "I'm a shortboarder." Maybe that's his way of trying for some independence, some separation. The better the mom and dad are at surfing, the more careful they must be to ensure they are gentle and not at all pushing their kids to surf, directly or indirectly.

More Kids' Issues

Let's hit a few more important highlights on successfully launching, enhancing, and maintaining your children's surfing lives. We emphasized the importance of the right surfboard. Equally important is to provide them with a quality, well-fitted wetsuit for cooler water. Nothing will kill a young person's interest and ability to have fun more quickly than physical discomfort, especially being cold or in pain. Follow the advice in Chapter 8 for acquiring a wetsuit with emphasis on having the patience to find one that fits perfectly, doesn't rub or restrict, isn't too tight, has no voids, and is not too loose. Wetsuits like this render your children impervious, buying them many wonderful hours in the water on cooler days that they'd never have otherwise. On pain prevention, strongly consider a helmet. This bolstered Ryan's confidence enough to take on rocky point breaks in the early going and helped him overcome what seems to be a fairly widespread (and perfectly sensible) fear of rocky bottoms among children learning to surf (Photo 9.8).

PHOTO 9.8 Ryan is a very comfortable, confident, and happy surfer, and his high-quality 3/2 Quiksilver wetsuit is a big part of that on a late winter afternoon in eastern Australia. It's well worth outfitting your kids with good equipment.

Photo by Matthew Bambling

Getting back to boogie boards for a moment, an important note is to buy your children protective socks and properly fitting fins with keeper straps to fix them securely to their ankles. They may balk at the extra gear in the early going, preferring just the board, no leash or other accessories, to mess around in small shore dump waves. It's never long, however, before they begin venturing farther afield and begin missing waves out beyond the whitewater because they are not wearing fins. We recommend not battling over the topic of wearing fins after you initially and very gently put a bug in their ear about the advantages. Simply bring the fins along in the beach bag, and let the children come to you for them. They're smart, they won't forget what you said, and they'll figure out on their own that they're costing themselves. They see what the bigger kids are doing with fins on, and they'll emulate them all on their own. Make it *their* idea. Coincidentally, you just happen to have the fins on hand when they're ready for them. Once they start using them, they'll never go without them.

Another issue that we must address is the prevalence of separated parents, and the very sad tendency of some to put selfishness and possessiveness ahead of their children's well-being. Whatever you do, don't be self-centered and stand in the way if the surf conditions are good and your ex happens to be the main surfing supervisor of the kids. Be flexible; let the kids enjoy the surfing. Consider making up the time on days when the surf is unsuitable. Or try getting more involved on the surfing front yourself. Don't obstruct children's surfing joy just because a court order says you can. Put the kids first.

Another corollary in the area of managing your children's well-being comes strongly into play with regard to surfing, and that is remembering that the biggest rewards you can ever give your children are your time and attention. By time and attention we mean your unconditional, unselfish love; your undivided focus; positive reinforcement; encouragement; consistency; dependability; and a gentle, guiding, supportive hand. Harshness, impatience, overinstructing, and biting criticism tear down, rather than build, confidence and a sense of self-worth. Chronically attempting to elicit desired behaviors through bribery using assorted cheap currencies—money, treats like sweets and soda and fast food, extra time on Play Station, or material possessions—is doomed to failure by the superficiality of the foundation. Your children value *you* and your attention far more than any of these things, or even more worthy material gifts. We challenge you to find a more binding, wholesome, healthy, and spiritual activity than taking your children surfing (Photo 9.9).

A few last tips before we move on:

PHOTO 9.9 Scott and Ryan stick together, in the surf and in life, through all kinds of conditions.

~ We'd make a very slight exception to the bribery wisdom in surfing and admit going to the straight bribe to overcome the odd hurdle. Selective, very limited, unpredictable, low-key use can be effective. Scott, for example, has taken Ryan to the beach on occasion in excellent conditions for him, only to have him uncharacteristically balk at the prospect of getting out through dumping shore waves. Standing side by side at the water's edge, "I can't get out, Dad." "Really?" "They look too big." "I'll be darned. They look a whole lot smaller than those ones last week. Tell you what, I don't think you'll have any trouble at all as good as you are, and I'll bet you a milk shake, hamburger, and a bucket of hot chips at Bella's Beach Café (Ryan's favorite), even with a two-minute head start, I can beat you to the take-off zone. You lose, you pay. Wouldn't blame you for not betting, because I'm planning to win." "Really?! Start on the count of three?" And they're off and they have a great session.

~ Don't be in any rush to surf side by side with your children, and think of kids' outings as just that—it's not about you, it's about them. You'll spend a few years in or near the whitewash, and you'll gaze out occasionally with a wistful sigh at guys and gals having a ball out beyond. Sure, you may be able to tag-team with a trusted spouse or friend and get out for a bit, and on selected days you may be able to match your equipment to your child's equipment and find a little spot "out the back" where you can both take off and surf. Characteristically this will be glassy and small, with either a partner hanging back with the children when you ride a wave and they don't, or a cluster of surfers you

PHOTO 9.10 Ryan, as shown here playing around at age seven, still hops on that 6′6″ foam board from time to time.

Photo by Herb McCormick

know keeping an eye on things. Ryan likes Scott to ride the same wave in more challenging conditions, so he's never far away, and if they're out alone Scott will pull off if he sees Ryan isn't catching the wave, or quickly catch the next wave by whatever means necessary if Ryan gets one and he misses. Scott knows one father who surfed virtually every day with his son from the age of five to seventeen.

~ Remember that first foam board, like Ryan's 6′6″? Don't get rid of it. Ryan, any time he is pushing the envelope of his comfort zone, will still take that board out for a few rides first, and then switch to a high-performance fiberglass board. And many, many of his schoolmates and friends, as we mentioned, have gotten started on it (Photo 9.10).

~ What if you've moved from inland to the coast, it's the entire family's first opportunity to try surfing, and no one knows where to begin? Or, one parent can surf but the kids are teenagers and will take advice better from someone else? Don't hesitate to sign them, or everyone, up for a surf school. There are tons of them in nearly every surfing area of any popularity, and by and large they do an outstanding job. It's money well spent and it can jump-start the whole process for you. Ask around and get recommendations if you can, and go for it.

What About the Ladies?

Some of the best surfers in the world are women. Many of the best amateur surfers at some locations are women, and some can surf better than most of the men on any given day. Admittedly, at the highest levels, it's like comparing the WNBA to the NBA, if only from the perspective of body mass, bone structure, musculature, and upper-body strength, but this is irrelevant. We see awe-inspiring women surfers regularly in local casual outings. While the ladies have come a long way in the modern era, they're still chasing the prominence of their Polynesian ancestral surfing matriarchs. We see them coming much further still in terms of their surf presence, year by year. Localism, the infamous practice of attempting to exclude nonregulars from a surf spot, has been chauvinistically extended in some cases to women. High male-to-female ratios still characterize many surfing areas.

Well, guys, get ready to move over some more. Having these lovely ladies, of all ages, with us out in the surf accentuates and gentles the entire atmosphere and makes everyone the better for it. We're all here together. The joy is so often in the sharing. Some women get out there on their shortboards and rip and carve just as hard as many of the men. Others give new meaning to the grace and economy of motion surfing a longboard. We all learn from each other. We all see things differently as they develop along a wave face, and we respond in our own special way. Women surfers are special, really special.

Why aren't there as many women out there surfing as men? They learn at least as quickly and they surf extremely well. One reason, worldwide, is suppression by society, so this answer to the surfing question is the same as the answer to the question of why aren't there a roughly equal proportion of women doing most everything else too? Because as adults they're kept barefoot, pregnant, and behind a frying pan? Pampered and given dolls instead of surfboards when they're little? In "developed" societies the suppression may take more subtle forms or it may in some cases have been largely removed, legally at least, yet it takes time for traditional roles and attitudes to change and for individuals to step out and fill that void. Janice Weaver surfs, and so does Scott's wife, Robyn McIntyre. How do we all go about getting more women involved? Wouldn't you men and women like to be out there together, instead of trying to accumulate enough brownie points so you can go alone?

The simple answer is to read this book and go surfing, whether you are a woman or a man, girl or boy. Obviously, applying the preceding instruction sequence about children equally to girls and boys is one solution. Let us add a few insights, though, specifically intended to help women. Let's say you are in your midthirties to midfifties, reasonably fit, comfortable in the water, a decent swimmer, and you live within striking distance of a coastline with some reasonably consistent surf. What can you do to tip the scales in your favor, give yourself a boost up the ladder? The first thing you, and any man reading this, can do is to work on your conditioning, flexibility, and body strength. Try following the programs described in *Fit to Surf* by Rocky Snyder. Rocky is a friend of Janice and Wingnut, and he knows the subject inside and out. Wingnut has another friend who simply fixes his leash to a nearby tree, places his surfboard in his swimming pool, and paddles in place. Scott's son Ryan places a "water skateboard"—an elongated oval of foam—under his chest and swims laps in their pool. This device encourages a head-up, identical stroke to paddling strongly on a shortboard. Either of these pool exercises works in quite a small swimming pool. The second thing you can do is practice your pop-ups, as recommended earlier, five to ten per day. Getting a little of all of these things going will sharply boost your ability to quickly be up, riding, and having a ball on your new surfboard.

What About Everyone?

Women, men, girls, boys—everyone—we can't overemphasize how effective following Wingnut's wisdom, as presented in this book, can be for you, and we humbly present this sequence of photos and words for your inspiration. They depict a true story. These photos were taken just two days before this manuscript went to the publisher. Ryan (who turned nine three days before this photo), his cousins Simon (age ten) and Olivia (age twelve), and their dad, Steve Bannerot (age forty-three), arrived in eastern Australia from their home in Seattle. None had ever touched a surfboard. They'd all watched *Endless Summer II* multiple times and dreamed of someday surfing. Luckily, the conditions were perfect the day they arrived. We simply followed the advice given in this book, and here's what happened.

We started out with pop-up practice straight off the plane, having grabbed the boards and made a beeline for that same perfect beginner's spot where Ryan got his first long rides at age three, featuring shallow sand bottom and gentle, small, spilling waves (Photo 9.11). We had the perfect choice of waves, we had perfect equipment, we had the perfect advice, all the right tips before we got in the water. So *then* what happened?

Surfing is truly for everyone, and these photos prove how easy it can be to get started. What are you waiting for?

PHOTO 9.11 Pop-up practice—that's Simon on that same old 6′6″ foam board of Ryan's, Steve on the grass, Scott kneeling, and Olivia looking on (a). Time to head out for a first try—Simon is on the 6′6″, and Olivia, closely attended by Scott, is on Robyn McIntyre's 9′ Robert August High Performance longboard (identical to the board depicted in Figure 4.2) (b). Incredibly, Simon is up and riding on his *very first wave*, having been pushed on by Scott (c). Steve gives Ryan, who is riding his custom 7′2″ longboard, a thumbs-up (note Steve is using Scott's 9′6″ Robert August WIR, identical to the board shown in Figure 4.2 except for color) (d). Riding well and effortlessly, Ryan inspires Olivia, Simon, and Steve. Olivia is up briefly on her first wave, and then takes a spill, having been pushed on by Scott (not visible), as Simon pushes through on his way back out to the take-off zone (e). On her second wave, Olivia is up and riding (f). Several waves later Olivia looks graceful and fluid, with the board in perfect trim, like she's been doing it for years (g). Here she goes again—Scott (not visible at left) has pushed her on, and she is very elegantly popping up as she surfs between Simon and Steve (h). And here she goes again, having been pushed on by Scott, with Ryan (sitting) and Simon looking on, and Steve (beyond her) paddling but looking like he'll miss this wave (i)—this is approximately the eighth wave of Olivia's life. The ride continues (j), a dream come true for a twelve-year-old young lady with access to superb equipment on waves perfect for her. Synergism—Ryan is up and riding, Olivia is popping up (having paddled on herself), as Steve smiles his approval (k). Olivia and Simon are surfing beautifully within the first twenty minutes of their surfing lives—thanks, Wingnut (l)! Olivia is already playing with turns, and Simon has intuitively mastered his weight distribution for maximum speed (m). On the very next wave, Ryan is cruising easily, Simon is heading back for the take-off zone, and Olivia has turned and decided to join Ryan—look at her lovely paddling form (n). Ryan begins to pull back as Olivia blissfully accelerates on the smooth, unbroken wave face toward a golden sunset (o). By the way, Steve got up and riding with ease too.

Photos by Robyn McIntyre

(continued)

Photos by Robyn McIntyre

Photos by Robyn McIntyre

(continued)

Photos by Robyn McIntyre

Photos by Robyn McIntyre

Teacher-Student Relationships

Regardless of who is teaching whom, we have touched on some of the sensitivities involved in what can be a delicate situation when the surf teaching relationship is between spouses or between parents and children. Here are some things to watch out for:

~ **Spousal and boyfriend/girlfriend relationships.** A high proportion of people don't take instructions well from their own spouse, for whatever reasons, most weaving back through years of interactions and complexities. Partners in newer relationships don't always fare much better. If this is the case, don't fight it—don't bring this kind of tension into your surfing life. Send the learner spouse to surf school or hire a private surf instructor as a birthday or Christmas present so he or she can get up to speed. Then you can surf together and avoid the teacher-student relationship altogether. You love each other; why not maximize the fun and avoid the tension?

~ **Child-parent relationships.** Don't feel bad if your preteen or teen takes advice better from your sibling, a friend, or peers when it comes to surfing, and don't hesitate to hire an instructor or sign your child up for surf school, same as above.

~ **Comfort zones.** If you are the experienced surfer, you may at times have difficulty fully comprehending how a given condition could possibly be intimidating to your spouse, friend, or children. Don't be judgmental. Just accept it, be gentle, and adopt the oft-expressed carefree philosophy of the Bahamas, a shrug and "next time, mon." Pushing, with the exception of the odd judicious bribe described earlier for children when you are quite certain they can handle it, will almost always do more harm than good. Find a different location with more suitable conditions. Or go do something else fun and wait for another day.

~ **Positive reinforcement.** Nothing is more important to the beginning surfer than positive reinforcement. There's always something to compliment, regardless of the performance. Anyone who is out there giving it a go deserves respect and encouragement. Helpful, constructive tips are important to sprinkle in very gently, but being upbeat and positive is crucial.

A surfing family is a cohesive, healthy, and happy family. If this accurately describes your family, everything else pales in comparison. You've got it all.

The Traveling Surfer

10

T he previous chapter got the whole family surfing. The logical next step: why not take a great family trip, or, if you have yet to start your own family, a great-group-of-friends trip, to a surfing destination? Whether a simple road trip up or down the coast or a big plane trip to an exotic locale, surfing constitutes an excellent centerpiece for enriching travel, not the kind of trip where you stand around and look at things, a trip that intimately immerses you, literally and figuratively, in the location. Combine surfing with other activities like SUP surfing, diving, swimming, snorkeling, kayaking, fishing, hiking, golf, photography, eco-touring, music, dancing, wine tasting, exotic cuisine, and culture . . . how can you miss?

It's fair to say that surfing lends itself perfectly to nomadic behavior on some scale. It's also fair to say that with a situation that ripe for instigation, Bruce Brown's 1964 creation *Endless Summer* permanently coalesced the notion of traveling to surf. Perhaps that's how it came to pass that populations of enthusiastic surfers living along more densely inhabited, affluent subtropical to temperate coastlines have developed a protocol of acquiring a regular tropical getaway. For Californians, this began with road trips to Mexico or the relatively short plane ride to places farther south, especially Costa Rica, or farther afield to the Mecca of all hard-core surfers, Hawaii. East Coast residents of the United States flee to the Caribbean, places like Puerto Rico, the Bahamas, and Barbados. Australians, accustomed to long plane rides to get anywhere, think nothing of regular surfing trips to places like Indonesia, the Maldives, Fiji, Papua New Guinea, Samoa, Tonga, Tahiti, and Pohnpei, and New Zealanders are much the same. Europeans frequent all of the above.

Wingnut is a perfect example. He first left home in California to surf Costa Rica during the filming of *Endless Summer II* in 1992 and, despite surfing all over the world for his professional work, he's been back every year since. That tells you something about the desirability of a lovely, environmentally rich, surfer-friendly foreign destination. In fact, a trip from North America to Costa Rica to go surfing constitutes an ideal template for Wingnut's general surf travel tips.

Making Surf Travel a Success

Wingnut's general travel protocol can be applied to virtually any surfing trip. We'll add more tips that apply to specific destinations in the next section, and medical considerations are covered in Appendix B (see also Chapter 6).

~ **Research the destination.** Where are the waves, and what are their characteristics, including size, shape, season of peak occurrence, and water temperature? What is the bottom composition of the surf spots, availability and mode of accommodation, food, transport, and alternative activities? What is the security situation? What special medical precautions may be prudent? Do you know someone with firsthand experience whom you can interview? No single facet of trip preparation is more important than educating yourself about the destination.

~ **Match your crew to the purpose, degree of required expertise, and characteristics of the destination.** Ask yourself what you expect from the specific trip, and who will fit in. Is this a family trip? What surf conditions suit the ages and abilities of your group? How can you distribute time among the available spots to satisfy the needs of everyone without exceeding comfort zones?

~ **Choose your crew wisely and be clear about your expectations.** Avoid any potential bad apples, people who have any tendency to be inflexible, be negative, sour easily, exert too much selfish control over others, handle unexpected conditions or events poorly, anger or become agitated easily, or be culturally insensitive or rude to others. Invite happy, relaxed, positive, enthusiastic, cheerful, adaptable, helpful people with broad comfort zones and easy-going natures. The more smiles, the better. Remember that a single bad apple can inordinately dampen the fun for all, while the synergism of a happy crew knows no limits.

~ **Institute crew policy understood by all.** Basically, keep up or shut up. If you get too cold, injured, or fatigued, or the conditions don't suit you, paddle in and relax on the beach, and do not interfere with or infringe on the enjoyment of others. Take pleasure in their fun if unable to participate yourself. Of course, in the case of families, the needs of all members must be catered tenderly, with empathy, gentleness, and love, and curtailment of full-on adult activities is an a priori condition of any outing. Kids come first.

~ **Select generalized boards.** Choose your surfboards carefully, with emphasis on those capable of surfing enjoyably the widest range of conditions. Wingnut typically chooses one very generalized board and one "hot dog board," in his case often more of a specialty noserider. Also check out destinations that have high-quality surfboards available by prearrangement, for example, Surftech's growing network, to avoid the hassle and expense of taking your own boards.

~ **Take a variety of fins.** Another prime way to cover a range of possible conditions is to take along a variety of fins that will enhance your ability to change the performance characteristics of your board to better suit the conditions of the day. For example, Wingnut would be very likely to pack the two boards described in Figure 8.1 and bring along at least a 9″ single fin for the Wingnut 2 (his more generalized board) and a 10″ single fin for the Wingnut Noserider.

~ **Purchase a high-quality, multiboard travel bag.** No point transporting your babies in a day bag, only to find them smashed upon arrival. Get a thick, purpose-built travel bag that will house two or more boards.

~ **Prepare your boards for travel.** Purchase lengths of split foam conduit insulation, designed to insulate refrigeration and other piping and widely available, and fit and tape sections around the nose and tail and along the rails. Remove the fins. Wrap beach towels around the tail block. Place everything in a travel bag.

~ **Bring soft racks.** Rental vehicles seldom come equipped with surfboard racks, so padded, highly portable soft racks, consisting of a long strap running through a padded section, which can be run through the passenger cab of a vehicle and up and around the roof and cinched tight, enable you to secure stacks of boards on the roof of your car. For longboards, strap them on the vehicle roof with the tail forward to minimize the force of wind resistance. All boards should be strapped on deck down.

~ **Bring ding repair kits.** The Surfco Hawaii kits described in Chapter 8 are perfect, right down to the fact that they are nonhazardous and airline-safe.

~ **Bring along a backup for everything.** Bring a second leash, sunglasses, sandals, sunscreen, and other essentials so loss of one critical link won't sideline you or detract from your ability to enjoy the trip. When it's time to return home, leave such extras behind for goodwill. In many destinations, items we take for granted are difficult to come by and will be deeply appreciated.

~ **Bring along a comprehensive first aid/medical kit.** This should be more advanced than a normal day kit and should be adjusted to the specific location and the availability of medical care—which is often very, very minimal. Please see Appendix B, Medical Considerations, for much more on the details of medical kits.

~ **Portable power and memory.** Be sure to organize and pack chargers, adapters to local power voltage, extra battery packs, extra digital camera memory cards, and memory sticks for downloading from camera via your own laptop or local computer.

~ **Set yourself up for minimal communications demands while on travel.** Check expected phone and e-mail capability and availability at your destination, and do what you can to curtail the expectations of others while you are away. Ask yourself how much time you really care to spend on e-mail and telephone while you are on this trip. Warning: Many island destinations claim to have e-mail capability, but the connections are so slow you may spend more time screen-watching than surfing. Tidy up affairs, leave some sort of phone message or divert to another number, and consider automated e-mail replies informing business associates and others of your absence and expected return.

~ **Maximize your exposure to the full adventure of your destination.** We mentioned the importance of researching alternative activities. No destinations have perfect surf conditions every day. Plan on partaking of other available activities, but not on an inflexible, prearranged basis, because inevitably the surf will be perfect on those days. Know the location and availability of local golf courses, tennis courts, charter fishing and diving boats, local attractions and tours, and "things to do and see." Make some inquiries, and let the operators know the dates you will be around and the tentative nature of your availability. Know where to go and what to do for those days when surf conditions are unsuitable. Select trips that permit you to adopt the attitude that even if there wasn't a single good day of surf, you'd still have a blast, and every good surfing day is just a bonus.

Travel Prospects and Perspectives

Surf travel has grown from rudimentary beginnings into a burgeoning industry, spreading rapidly in terms of destinations; modes of execution; degree of specialization; and availability of high-quality, on-site boards and other equipment, yet cutting-edge experiences and breaks never surfed are still possible, and adventurous souls are out there pushing the envelope as you read this. Surfing is fundamentally nonconsumptive, is ecologically benign, and requires relatively little on-site infrastructure. Hence many top-rated surf camps consist of simple screened huts or bungalows right on the beach, with a communal eating area and shared restroom and shower facility. This keeps it low-key and low cost. You paddle out to the break right in front of your hut for as long as you feel like it. No problem, mon. The camp will usually have boats to transport you farther afield. At the other end of the spectrum, equally impressive surf breaks are now serviced by luxury accommodations that offer gourmet fare, air-conditioned en suite palaces, and day boat trips or longer live-aboard boat sojourns. Most surf resorts have guides available. Packages vary widely in all aspects. Some destinations feature a wide variety of breaks suitable for a wide range of skills. More often the flavor of a specific destination, however, is oriented to a narrower category of surfing skill.

Let's give a few specific examples so you can get your feet wet. As with our treatment of surfboards, we point out that the spectrum of possible surfing destinations is vast and the place to wander widely is the Internet. For instance, check out "List of Surfing Areas" on Wikipedia (http://en.wikipedia.org/wiki/List_of_surfing_areas), and you'll find seventeen pages of destinations, and this list doesn't even scratch the surface. The list omits entire nations full of spots (and they readily acknowledge this and invite all of us to contribute). Anyway, you get the picture. We'll start with some selected samples to illustrate helpful perspectives.

First, one very common tendency is for surfers to be critical of the surf at their home location. Maybe they've seen too many highlight films of other breaks around the world, films that of course do not include all of the "bad" days (go to the surfline.com surf cam at Pipeline much of the time outside the peak season and it's flat—you'd never know it was the world's most famous power tube wave). Wingnut has done a great deal of professional work in Japan, and he constantly repeated this refrain to his apologetic Japanese hosts. Scott hears the same thing along the coast of Australia, local surfers frequently making less-than-flattering comments about the surf. Local pro and topnotch shaper Marty Simpson (Black Widow Surfboards and Surfboards Australia) was speaking to Scott recently about this very topic, saying, "People around here are always talking about the lack of power and consistency of our Sunshine Coast surf, yet I had a group here from California for a week of quite average conditions and they were absolutely raving about it. Locals don't properly value what we have." The moral of the story is twofold: (1) appreciate your own surf break; (2) don't hesitate to expand your horizons.

The second bit of perspective is a corollary to the first. Don't underestimate the impact of surfing a new area on your set of skills, ideas, and development. Wingnut gives the classic example of the difference between California, his home break, and Hawaii, a place he visits and surfs often. The Hawaiian style of longboarding is a direct outgrowth of locals adjusting to the generally more powerful waves. They tend to be "looser" and more progressive, driving and maneuvering harder and faster, avoiding the impact zone so they don't get thumped, but still imposing their will on the areas of the wave that allow them to do so. Californians tend to have a longboard style that matches the generally weaker, slower waves. They typically have more time—they fade, stall, cut back, and set up frequent nose rides—and they have the option of spending more time surfing in a traditional, as opposed to a progressive, style. Hawaii locals feature many *switch masters*, those able to surf equally well in a *goofy* or *regular* foot stance, allowing them to orient frontside on lefts or rights. This ability is not as common in California—there's less imperative for developing the skill.

Applying these surfing perspectives to specific examples, let's look at a new, very remote surf camp that features a variety of waves from soft longboard conditions to sizable tubes, Nusa Island Retreat in Papua New Guinea (nusaislandretreat.com.pg; promotional DVD *Surfing PNG* available from worldsurfaris.com). The natural beauty of the area, its amenability to a range of surfing skills, and the opportunity to advance those skills from spilling waves to tube riding have this destination fully booked up to eighteen months in advance. This spot also emphasizes the need to fully research and consider medical precautions, as visitors are at risk of cerebral malaria and should definitely take recommended prophylactics prior to the trip. Here surfers live in simple accommodations at the camp and mostly take day boat trips to the breaks. The locals are Melanesian, strongly traditional with varying degrees of Christian overlay.

Hopping over to the Indian Ocean, let's take a look at the Maldives, an isolated archipelago of lovely coral atolls located southwest of India in the remote open ocean. The majority of surfing packages feature multiple-day live-aboard boat trips. Purpose-built, displacement-hull power cruisers and efficient sail-assisted yachts with all the amenities ferry surfers and their families to assorted out islands. Degree of difficulty varies, right up to some hollow reef breaks with tube sections best suited to advanced surfers. Opportunities for beachcombing, swimming, kayaking, windsurfing, snorkeling, and scuba diving comprise most of the range of alternative activities. The prices vary fairly widely depending on the operation and the degree of privacy and creature comforts desired. The Maldives are predominantly Muslim. They did experience a recent terrorist bombing, although the general degree of security and local friendliness is still considered good. Again, worldsurfaris.com will send you a promotional DVD, and many other surf travel companies market this destination (two examples are atolltravel.com and globalsurfguides.com).

We've discussed Costa Rica, with its laid-back, Spanish-speaking Latin culture, strongly Christian population, very safe security, surfer-friendliness across the board, low costs, and large variety of surf breaks for every skill level. Wingnut outlines his favorite destinations, accommodations, boat trip possibilities, and protocol in the *Wingnut's Art of Longboarding* DVD series, and we'll let you soak it all in from that source. Wingnut and Robert August actually guide groups at these locations fairly often, so if you'd like to go with the pros check out details at robertaugust.com or gowithapro.com.

What about a premier destination that covers every imaginable skill level, from absolutely frightening waves for experts only down to friendly beach breaks, a place so vast and with so much variety that several lifetimes would be required to fully experience it? Throw in availability of high-quality surfboard rentals, a huge variety of live-aboard boat trips to remote island groups, shore accommodations from diminutive and dirt-cheap to the most luxurious you could ever want, indisputably some of the very best surf in the world, and an exotic local mix of cultures and cuisine, and you have landed squarely in Indonesia, in the heart of the Indo-Pacific. This is at the opposite end of the spectrum from Costa Rica, densely populated and mostly Muslim and inevitably frenetic at the population centers. Here again, a couple of isolated although severe terrorist bombings have failed to suppress the general goodwill between locals and foreign visitors. Politics and crowds will be the last thing on your mind if you hop aboard one of the surfer's yacht trips to the Mentawai Islands, off the coast of Sumatra, where you can enjoy tranquil remote areas with some of the most beautiful tubes in the world. Rather than list one or several of the many operations catering to this area, we will simply recommend a one-stop shop, Aussie Peter Neely's Indo Surf (indo surf.com.au, surfbooks.biz), an extremely comprehensive and frequently updated guidebook to virtually everything you could ever want to know about a surf trip to this nation of roughly 17,000 islands, with stunning photography.

Wherever you decide to go, remember that a smile and some up-front respect will carry you a long way. Cultural awareness is paramount. Learn about local customs before you go, and practice a bit of the language. Attempts to converse, however rudimentary, are immediately appreciated almost everywhere. Bring those extras, and give them all away when you leave. Be a good example, a good ambassador.

The Ultimate Dream

Well, you may have guessed where all this is leading. We're building your dream of surfing success, block by block. We've provided a blueprint that encompasses everything you need to succeed, and we just finished whetting your appetite for a little surf travel. Many tropical surf destinations now offer live-aboard boat tours. You fly in, get transported to the boat, stay for a fairly short time, then get back on a plane and go home. We only go around once, as far as anyone seems to know for sure; we can't take money with us; and when it's time to go, well, we don't have any more time. And, as the saying goes, the older you get, the more dead people you know. We all have reflective moments—what-ifs, you might call them. What if you had the money, and the time? What would you do?

Once upon a time (February 1996), Scott and several fellow sailors borrowed Kim Andersen's trusty old pickup truck and drove to the windward side of lonely, extremely remote Christmas Island—the one that belongs to the Republic of Kiribati, and is located about 2 degrees north of the equator, about 870 nautical miles due south of Hawaii's Big Island. Both crews had sailed to this outpost on their own sailboats, Scott's forty-one-foot sloop *Elan*, and Jens Yeager and Allyson Madsen's forty-two-foot ketch *Indigo*, from French Polynesia to avoid South Pacific hurricane (or cyclone) season. They wished to see the sights and have a picnic at this deserted portion of the world's largest coral atoll (in terms of land mass). Lo and behold, upon arrival to the most isolated part of the island they spotted this guy sitting out there on a motorcycle. He gave a friendly wave and they pulled up alongside him. Eric Vogt, in his forties, was visiting from Kauai, Hawaii, waiting for the surf to come up. He got a lot more interested when he learned they had inflatable dinghies and lived aboard sailboats, and he asked if anyone was interested in surfing. Jens and Scott both volunteered that they were, Eric joined them for lunch, and they set up an outing for the next day.

The next morning Scott and Jens picked up Eric and his board. Scott brought an old single-fin shortboard kindly given to him by Mike Owens when he visited Scott a few months prior in Tahiti. Soon Jens, Eric, and Scott were dropping anchor outside a hollow reef break in the middle of the main pass into the vast lagoon of the island. A good swell was running, and each time a wave came in and sucked up water into its face, whole coral heads poked treacherously out of the water in front of the steep aqua walls. Before the anchor hit bottom Eric donned a sun hat and launched prone off the dinghy with his surfboard, paddled straight onto the first wave arriving, took off, and went zipping along, weaving between exposed coral heads, then paddled back out laughing at having surfed right over the back of a large reef shark (a "heavy local," he said). He never even got his hat wet. Jens and Scott couldn't believe it. This led to a series of outings, Eric taking Scott under his wing and sending him his first real surfboard when he returned to Hawaii, an 8′2″ fun board. But it also led to something else. Eric got really excited about what Scott was doing, taking a sabbatical from his Florida charter business to attempt a "working circumnavigation" aboard his sailboat. All Eric could think about was the plethora of unpopulated surf breaks and the lifestyle. To make a long story short, Eric returned to Kauai, sold his business, married a great gal named Tammy, bought a thirty-seven-foot steel cutter in California, named it *Naia*, and they surfed and sailed their way all over Central America and the tropical Pacific. A decade later Eric, Tammy, and their lovely daughter, Mahina, still live aboard and surf, currently in New Zealand.

We've also mentioned T. C. Cardillo and Paul McGrew, and their similar execution of an extensive boat-based traveling surf plan. Scott met them in the Marshall Islands (Micronesia) shortly after they'd completed the refit of their spacious trimaran *Cherokee* during free time from their jobs in connection with the U.S. military installation at Kwajalein Atoll. These guys and assorted crew sailed widely in the South Pacific, as far south as New Zealand, and then worked their way back to Hawaii, surfing countless unnamed locations.

You may recall being introduced to Californian brothers Andrew and Chris Krajacic earlier in the book when they accosted Scott at Musket Cove Resort, Fiji, and gleefully forced him to come out and try his new board at Wilke's Pass, just north of Tavarua. Drew, scant months before, at age twenty-three had been recently laid off a high-powered accounting job secured shortly after graduation, and he decided to sell his newly purchased house rather than continue to be a slave to a fat monthly mortgage payment. Soon after, he and his twenty-six-year-old brother, Chris, purchased a thirty-one-foot 1968 Cheoy Lee ketch with wood spars, classic lines, and an aging eighteen-horsepower diesel for $16,000 and christened it *Crackerjack*.

Both accomplished surfers, they'd never sailed but figured they'd learn soon enough. They had never even raised sail on the boat—just did everything they could to prepare the boat, bought provisions, loaded their surfboards, and headed straight from Santa Barbara for Maui. Scott met them, months later, in Apia, Samoa, just before they departed the harbor for a little surfing trip around the eastern tip of Upolu, and then turned west along the famed south shore. Busily poring over surf guides, under full power and sail downwind in glassy conditions, a long, slow swell lifted the boat, heeling her just enough to send their treasured lone piece of navigation equipment, a hand-held GPS, clattering overboard with a splash. Both brothers launched simultaneously overboard, missing the GPS, with *Crackerjack* racing away. Drew lunged for the dinghy towing in the wake and just grabbed it, but during a lengthy struggle to pull himself to the transom of the ketch, he swamped and snapped the tow line. Now separated from Chris, and two miles out in the blue ocean, he dispiritedly struck out swimming for the island. He said his main disappointment was the loss of the boat and their dream. He was in excellent condition, reasonably naïve about the strength and danger of the pre-vailing offshore current, and confident he'd make land. Periodically he sadly looked up to see *Crackerjack*, still flying along on autopilot, getting smaller and smaller on the horizon.

On one such glance, he noticed the boat had swung around and was heeled over—improbably grounded on the seaward-most projection of the south shore reef. He immediately changed course and began swim-ming as rapidly as he could the three quarters of a mile or so to the boat. Again, to make a long story short, Chris also eventually made it to the boat, and with the help of local Samoans they got it unstuck and back afloat with survivable damage. They told me the story, among numerous other mishaps and adventures, when we remet in Fiji. They later survived a severe storm off the coast of Australia and made it in to Mooloolaba, Queensland, where Scott met them again upon arrival aboard *Elan*. They sold *Crackerjack* in Australia, continued surfing mostly in Costa Rica, and the last e-mail Scott got from them they were crewing on another sailboat and surfing in Tahiti. That's livin' large.

Young, strong, rich in adventurous spirit, mechanically talented, and self-reliant, Drew and Chris didn't let lack of money and experience get in their way. Their reward was a lifetime, and yes, at times, a life-threatening, experience. Rest assured that growing numbers of folks are taking to the world's oceans in far more substantial vessels, methodically prepared and with considerable safety margins. Many of the crews are families with young children. Having spent nearly nine years in this mode, including three with Ryan, Scott can't imagine a more idyllic lifestyle, particularly for those who can organize a sufficient financial base first. Scott was intermediate in this regard between the *Crackerjack* crew and the often older, more affluent retired couples sometimes equipped with open ocean luxury trawlers or larger, more expensive sailboats.

The questions become, "Do I wait until I really have it made and can well and truly afford it, say age sixty-five, and then do it?" versus "Gee, I'm still fit and fairly financially secure in my midthirties; I know I can afford a seaworthy forty-footer with all the right electronics and gear. Should I sacrifice a decade or so of prime earning years to go now while I can physically do it all?" In other words, what is the most important kind of wealth, a vastly enriched lifetime experience, or money . . . and how much money is enough to comfortably ensure financial security?

The sacrifices necessary to cut ties to land are substantial, although with advances in real-time communications the world is a much smaller place now. You can be in contact daily with friends and family from any-where on the earth. Nonetheless, don't underestimate the effort and time involved with being your own mechanic, plumber, electrician, and jack-of-all-trades while out away from port. As far as the children, they'll absolutely love it until they are at least into their young teens and hormones and social prerogatives kick in. With regard to finding the right woman or man for the extended sailing trip, it would be accurate to say that the desire not to nest-build in conventional society will narrow the field considerably, and that it will do so more for women than men. Nevertheless, there are many fine people out there willing to take the plunge, and in finding one of them you will likely discover many other attributes compatible with the surfing and sailing adventure of a lifetime.

What if, for assorted practical reasons, you really can't take the full plunge, prevented, perhaps, by responsibilities for others over which you have no control? No problem, cheat: there's a lot to be said for the many worldwide sailboat charter operations, like Sunsail and The Moorings. You can fly in to the most exotic areas of the world, load your surfboards and gear on board, turn the key, and be off on a week of surfing and adventure at least as good as those who are doing it on their own, with virtually none of the sacrifice. Yes, you'll need to take a sailing course before you do it, but that's no big deal. Alternatively, of course, you can go on one of the myriad surf destination boat charters and not have to lift a finger or raise a sail, just focus on surfing. In either case you can take that ten-day to four-week sojourn and jet right back to the security of home and job, bright-eyed and refreshed, and get back out to your home surf breaks the next afternoon straight out of work.

However you consummate your surfing life, the driving force inside you is that same spirit that made surfing such a central pillar of ancient Polynesian society: love of the ocean, the sensation of pure, unadulterated fun, and the willingness to share it with others. Of these metaphysical qualities, the willingness to share, more than any other, epitomizes the heart and soul of the surfing spirit. Sharing within a lineup, sharing a surf spot, sharing wave knowledge, sharing your expertise with children, friends, neighbors—the more fun-loving, happy, smiling people out there, the better and more enjoyable for everyone. This book is our humble contribution to the surfing spirit, and it is our sincere hope that it will assist you all in your journey.

Appendix A

We commented early on the existence of numerous alternative surfing vehicles to stand-up surfboards. Starting with the boogie board, suggested as an excellent precursor and complement to stand-up surfing, we can expand the discussion to two other stand-up board-riding modes applicable to surf, windsurfing and kite surfing. Both utilize wind as the primary source of propulsion, as opposed to wave energy, and then apply their trajectories either with or against wave faces. As such neither practice depends on "good surf," or for that matter any waves at all, and, importantly, ideal conditions for these practitioners are often poor conditions for surfing, for example, hard onshore winds. Conditions that depress a stand-up surfer often elate a kite surfer or wind surfer. Therefore, if you both surf and kite or wind surf, you might never be sad!

Two other surfing vehicles, kneeboards and rescue boards, require the rider to kneel rather than stand. Kneeboards are an exaggeration of the stand-up fish surfboard (and in fact the fish evolved from the kneeboard), short and wide. The rider wears fins and usually webbed gloves, kicking and paddling in a prone position to catch the waves, then pops up to a kneeling position. The bottom and top turns, reentries, and cutbacks are extremely similar to those performed on a stand-up shortboard, and the compact profile fits nicely in deep, hollow wave sections. Rescue boards, on the other hand, are thick, torpedo-shaped vehicles developed for surf life-saving. The rider kneels head down, butt up, and paddles in synchronized two-hand strokes to catch the wave, then leans and inserts a hand into the water to turn. The relatively large size and volume of these vehicles limits their maneuverability on wave faces but enhances their wave-catching ability. They can generally catch waves much earlier than a longboard.

Riders operate a variety of surf vehicles from a sitting position, including kayaks, assorted outrigger canoes, and various forms of wave skis and surf skis designed for surfing, ranging from relatively short, wide *goat boats* to elongated forms with a relatively high bow and tapered tail. Propulsion for all is a single- or double-ended paddle. The power and hull speed of these vehicles permits wave capture well before any paddle-on surfers, as well as the ability to capitalize on nonbreaking, long-wavelength swells unavailable to stand-up surfers because of insufficient hull speed. Thus, some of these vehicles can operate happily well outside and beyond the stand-up surfers, on waves they will never use. On the other hand, these vessels can also surf well in steeper breaking waves, which can and does bring them into conflict with stand-up surfers. By and large a little consideration and respect is all that is required to keep some separation and for users of one style of surf vehicle not to abuse other surfers with the specific characteristics of their gear (such as not taking all the waves before the paddle-on surfers have a chance).

Another increasingly popular practice that allows stand-up surfers to catch fast-moving, very large swells impossible to paddle on is tow-in surfing, where a personal watercraft (PWC, usually a Jet Ski or WaveRunner) tows the surfer into position on the wave face, the surfer drops the tow line as the board gains momentum from the building wave, then he or she rides normally. Originally developed on the North Shore of Oahu by Laird Hamilton and compadres Darrick Doerner and Buzzy Kerbox to gain access to big ocean swells breaking on offshore reefs, and also to avoid the paddle-on crowds, this practice has spread to smaller waves and in some cases brings tow-in surfers into conflict with paddle-on surfers. Early attempts used inflatables and other boats, and nowadays beginning tow-in surfers are again using these classes of boats in small surf. Like other alternatives to standard paddle-on, stand-up surfing, tow-in surfing at its best distributes surfers into places and conditions not previously utilized, most significantly onto enormous waves (more than sixty-five feet) too fast for "manual" capture. The surfboards and associated equipment at this upper end of the tow-in spectrum have become more specialized, first with foot straps to keep the rider from being bounced off by the chop on the giant wave faces, and then with the development of the *foilboard*. This device consists of a sort of ultrathin, small shortboard-like platform with a vertical strut fitted to horizontal wings. The rider is fixed in place by clamp-in ski-style boots, towed up to speed, levitating above the water surface, riding the wave perched above and over the foil wings. Commercial versions of this equipment became available in the early 2000s. The lack of drag permits smooth rides above wind chop and confers the ability to stay with the wave, introducing the possibility of riding long-wavelength, unbroken storm swells "indefinitely" in the open ocean.

Hey, what about us regular folks looking to expand our horizons? Well, enter the latest development, stand-up paddle (SUP) surfing (Photo 1). SUP surfboards are generally wider and longer than longboards. In fact, they're just oversized longboards, at least 28″ wide for beginners, 11′ to 12′ long, and often fitted with a full-length traction pad. The rider stands at all times, propelling the board with a single-ended paddle. SUP surfers can ride anything that a longboarder can ride and much, much more because of the greater hull speed and enhanced propulsion power conferred by the paddle. The real fun comes from being able to get out there and truly enjoy subpar conditions, riding tiny waves and waves that break, back off, and then break again. There's almost no flat section you can't make it through. Like other alternative vehicles, this surfing mode vastly expands the range of exploitable conditions, which translates into more fun and better physical conditioning with cross-training advantages to boot. Wingnut and Janice use them as a tandem board for kids, and many SUP surfers take their dogs out when the conditions are flat. Wingnut frequently goes fishing while he is out on his SUP board. If you've decided

PHOTO 1 Wingnut SUP surfing.

Duke Brouwer

to try for the "ultimate dream" described in Chapter 10—taking your own surfing journey on your own boat—imagine the advantages of using a SUP surfboard for a dinghy, getting from your vessel to the shore, dock, or bar, high and dry, no sitting in a wet vehicle. Scott's SUP surfing friends also take advantage of the fact that with no body parts in the water, they have more freedom to push the geographical and temporal limits of shark safety.

Of all the alternative vehicles, Wingnut's unequivocal favorite is SUP surfing. It reflects the philosophy of having more surfing fun on a day in, day out basis. It makes sense to maximize the amount of joy you can have on the ocean. Flat surf doesn't faze Wingnut one bit. The smile as he unloads his new SUP surfboard is just as wide.

Appendix B

Medical considerations begin with researching the intended surfing destination. The U.S. Centers for Disease Control and Prevention (CDC) at cdc.gov (under "Travelers' Health") is a great place to start, and CDC personnel are exceedingly helpful on the phone. Check out what vaccinations you should get for the particular area of the world you intend to visit. While malaria, yellow fever, and other high-profile afflictions seem to attract the most attention, many more mundane priorities are often overlooked. For example, make sure you have had a tetanus booster within the past ten years. The relatively new hepatitis vaccinations are also highly recommended. Check out the safety of consuming local water, and remember the axiom regarding water, raw vegetables, and fruit: if you don't peel it, boil it, or bleach it yourself, don't consume it. This helps protect you from numerous serious ailments, including gut infections, some forms of hepatitis, worms, cholera, and more exotic afflictions like parasitic meningitis.

All surfers should carry a first-aid kit, from a minimal day kit to the floating hospital advisable for long-range do-it-yourself boat trips. Here are some things to consider when you are putting together your kit. Your doctor can provide the prescriptions needed for these materials, and a pharmacist can either order them or direct you to the appropriate medical suppliers, as needed:

~ **Wound dressings.** All surfers should pack an assortment of bandages, including the superb Elastoplast dressings, nonstick pads, Steri-Strips, and padding tape for those who react to the sticking agent in standard adhesive bandages. Women's sanitary pads are an excellent absorptive component highly useful for compression and other bandages and much cheaper than the specialized options. You'll also need rolls of crepe bandaging wrap to secure dressing on larger wounds.

229

- **Wound cleaning materials.** Gloves, antiseptic solution (Betadine is hard to beat), gauze pads, cotton balls, and an unused spare toothbrush.
- **Wound debris extraction tools.** A selection of sterile hypodermic needles is superior to tweezers for removing debris, and they double as useful tools for cutting and lancing boils. Scalpels are also useful for lancing and for trimming jagged wound edges prior to suturing if no medical facilities are nearby.
- **Suturing materials.** Needles and thread for closing wounds on-site in remote areas.
- **Antibiotic ointments.** Bacteroban (Mucipurin) and Betadine are good choices.
- **Drawing salve.** Ichthammol and similar ointments, smeared on dressings along with antibiotic ointments, exert considerable osmotic extraction power for debris and pus in puncture wounds and infected areas and can work wonders overnight.
- **Oral antibiotics suitable for wounds.** Flucloxacillin may be the top choice.
- **Oral, nonsedating antihistamines.** These will reduce the effect of stings.
- **Skin salve for burns and stings.** Silvadene is a top selection for burns and also serves as a soothing, general antiseptic cream.
- **Pain relief.** Paracetomol and Nurofen tablets, or stronger medicines like Paracetomol with codeine if you can get them, are important for alleviating discomfort and allowing rest and healing to take place.
- **Standard ear drops.** For prevention and treatment of minor external ear infections, with active ingredients alcohol and acetic acid.
- **Antibiotic ear drops.** For ear infections.
- **Antibiotic eye ointment or drops.** For eye infections.
- **Saline solution.** Either ready-made from the pharmacy or created on-site by boiling water and salt, this is an excellent wash for eyes and general wounds.
- **Antifungal creams and powders.** If you sit around in damp board shorts much or stay wet much of the time in the tropics, sooner or later you'll experience the exquisite discomfort of crotch and butt crack inflammation. Once established, it can be hard to dislodge, and in its more virulent forms, it can cause crimson-red patches that itch so badly it can drive you crazy—and usually in areas you can't scratch the way you'd like in public. Many over-the-counter antifungal creams and powders exist, and you'll know very quickly whether or not your particular fungus is going to yield, shortly after application. If the itching continues to rage, switch to the next option. Scott got a really stubborn fungus in Micronesia that finally succumbed to Econazole Nitrate Cream (1%) mixed with Fluocinonide Cream to alleviate the

burning and itching. They're available by prescription only, and he never travels without them now.

~ **Antinausea and antidiarrhea medications, and electrolyte rehydration packs.** For prevention of dehydration and complications by alleviation of primary symptoms and replacement of fluids. Simple diarrhea kills many children annually worldwide and if untreated can become serious for anyone.

The farther afield you plan to venture, and particularly if you are constructing a medical kit for a long-range cruise, the larger and rarer the assortment of ailments and injuries you should prepare for. Examples of medicines to bring include Metronidazole (effective on the anaerobic organisms responsible for appendicitis), as well as a wider range of antibiotics, including selections intended for urinary tract infections, gut infections, and dewormers (Mebendazole). You'll want splints, slings, and triangular bandages. Defibrillators are becoming more and more common on private cruising vessels. One group of record-seeking blue-water spearfishermen charters Scott's friend, Captain Steve Campbell, in Tonga. Several are doctors, and they bring items like cutting-edge, ready-mix putty material for quickly sealing amputations. So, there's really no limit to what you might have on hand. It's very important to work closely with a competent physician when you design a medical kit suited to your needs. This treatment is by no means comprehensive, but it should provide a good start. And, as Wingnut says, going overboard just a bit on the medical kit seems to help ensure it's not needed.

Appendix C

Numerous video, Internet, and printed resources assisted the preparation of this book, and we mentioned many throughout the text. If we had to name a single most comprehensive reference and source of general and historical knowledge for surfers, it would be *The Encyclopedia of Surfing* by Matt Warshaw (2005, Harcourt, ISBN 0-015-603251-1). We highly recommend it to every one of you. *Learn to Surf for Beginners* (2003, ISBN 0-9751523-0-0) and *Learn to Surf Intermediate Level* (2004, ISBN 0-9751523-1-9), both compiled by the Academy of Surfing Instructors (an Australian-based group, academyofsurfing.com), provide clear, step-by-step instructions and information mostly from a shortboard perspective, and an advanced-level manual is supposed to emerge soon. Any surfer can benefit from *Fit to Surf* by Rocky Snyder (2003, Ragged Mountain Press/McGraw-Hill, ISBN 0-07-141953-5). Ladies, try *Sister Surfer: A Woman's Guide to Surfing with Bliss and Courage* by Kia Afcari and Mary Osborne (2005, Lyons Press, ISBN 1-59228-721-2). There's also a somewhat dated self-published work that still provides considerable detail on aspects of surfboard construction and performance, *Essential Surfing* by George Orbelian (1987, Orbelian Arts, ISBN 0-9610548-2-4).

Internet resources on surfing are vast. For general information across the board and for webcams, surfline.com is arguably the most comprehensive, and surfing.com is worth a look. Smaller examples more focused on checking the surf include coastalwatch.com and swellnet.com.au. For getting your feet wet in the area of self-forecasting, check out the resources at http://weather.noaa.gov, bom.gov.au, and metservice.co.nz. See world surfaris.com and liquiddestination.com as an entrée to surf destination websites (and note the website referrals in Chapter 10). For equipment, the massive surftech.com is an excellent introduction to a wide range of surfboards, SUP boards, all kinds of other items, and a who's who of major shapers. You can then go to the individual shaper's websites to see their full range of custom boards. See stumpysurf.com for an example of a top-notch shaper, international guide, and surfer. Other major manufacturer sites include oneill.com, quiksilver.com, ripcurl.com, and billabong.com.au. For surfing history, check out surfingheritage.org, clubofthewaves.com, surfingforlife.com, surfart.com, and surfing-art.com. For those of you ignited by the idea of setting sail and seeking the ultimate surfing dream, go to setsail.com, click on "sailor's logs," and see the perspectives of many experienced sailors (click on "Scott and Ryan Bannerot" for their ideas), and much more valuable information and other resources around the site.

Wingnut remains for Scott in a category of his own. He created his own niche in the world of surfing from the launch pad provided by *Endless Summer II*, the sequel to *Endless Summer*. He never bothered to surf the pro tours. He became the quintessential traveling surfer celebrity and ambassador of all that is good about the sport, and he played a dominant role in bringing the joy of longboarding back into focus for millions of surfers and potential surfers. This didn't happen through marketing facades and smoke and mirrors; it happened because of his unbelievable surfing skills, humility, grace, and sense of humor, and because he doesn't take himself too seriously. In other words, he's got soul. People sense it, even from a distance. His DVD series *Wingnut's Art of Longboarding 2 in 1,* and *Wingnut's Art of Longboarding 3: The Quest for Style*, form the basis for much of the material in this book. These DVDs are widely regarded as the best presentation ever created on exactly how to make some of the things he does on waves happen for you. It's Wingnut live and direct. Scott also highly recommends the lighthearted *Wingnut's Search for Soul*. His starring roles in *Endless Summer Revisited, Step into Liquid*, and *Chasing Dora* will please all Wingnut fans. Purchase all of these video products through either Amazon.com or robertaugust.com, or go to thesurfnetwork.com for instant downloads. If you'd like to go surfing with Wingnut at some of his favorite haunts in Costa Rica, go to gowithapro.com, and also keep an eye on robertaugust.com. For an incredibly comprehensive list of surf movies, videos, and DVDs in general, you must see Appendix 3 of Matt Warshaw's *The Encyclopedia of Surfing* to believe it (and, for that matter, Appendix 1 for surfing books and Appendix 4 for surf magazines).

One last thing, and we admit to being quite embarrassed about actually promoting Play Station for kids (strict time limits!), but we must tip our hats to *Kelly Slater's Pro Surfer,* and the other two in the series,

Sunny Garcia's Pro Surfing and *Transworld Pro Surfing*. *Kelly Slater's* in particular is a great primer on all the shortboard moves for the up-and-coming kids (and anyone else good enough to contemplate them). You can also do realistic virtual surfing almost anywhere in the world by going to youriding.com. And we've got to mention the DVD *Surf's Up*. Yeah, it's animated and it's very light, but a few of the scenes capture the flavor of actual spots in the heart of the tropical Pacific so well, if you've actually been there, it's almost eerie. Aloha.

Index